MUSKETTOE POINTE FARM

Robert Carter Ball

AMERICAN
FAMILY STYLE

AMERICAN
FAMILY STYLE

TEXT AND PHOTOGRAPHS BY

MARY RANDOLPH CARTER

FOREWORD BY

RALPH LAUREN

DESIGN BY

MARCIA WEINBERG

VIKING
STUDIO
BOOKS

VIKING STUDIO BOOKS

Published by the Penguin Group
Viking Penguin, a division of Penguin Books USA Inc.,
375 Hudson Street, New York, New York 10014, U.S.A.
Penguin Books Ltd, 27 Wrights Lane,
London W8 5TZ, England
Penguin Books Australia Ltd, Ringwood,
Victoria, Australia
Penguin Books Canada Ltd, 2801 John Street,
Markham, Ontario, Canada L3R 1B4
Penguin Books (N.Z.) Ltd, 182–190 Wairau Road,
Auckland 10, New Zealand

Penguin Books Ltd, Registered Offices:
Harmondsworth, Middlesex, England

First published in the United States of America by
Viking Penguin Inc. 1988
Published in Penguin Books 1990

1 3 5 7 9 10 8 6 4 2

Grateful acknowledgment is made for permission
to reprint "Solitude" from *Now We Are Six* by A. A. Milne.
Copyright 1927 by E. P. Dutton, renewed 1955 by A. A. Milne.
Reprinted by permission of Dutton Children's Books,
a division of Penguin Books USA Inc.,
Methuen Children's Books and McClelland and Stewart, Toronto.

The photographs on pages 11, 164, and 165 (two middle) appear
courtesy of *Self*, copyright © 1982 by The Conde Nast Publications Inc.

LIBRARY OF CONGRESS CATALOGING IN PUBLICATION DATA
Carter, Mary Randolph.
American family style: decorating, cooking, gardening,
entertaining/text and photographs by Mary Randolph Carter;
foreword by Ralph Lauren; design by Marcia Weinberg.
p.   cm.
ISBN 0 14 01.4489 7
1. Carter family.   2. Country life—United States.   3. United
States—Social life and customs—1971–   4. United States—Biography.
5. Cookery, American.   6. Interior decoration—United States.
7. Gardening—United States.   I. Title.
CT274.C365C374   1990
640.973—dc20   90–37874

Printed in the United States of America
Designed by Marcia Weinberg

For my mother and father and all my family,
but especially for Howard, Carter, and Sam.

CONTENTS

F A L L

W I N T E R

SPRING

SUMMER

FOREWORD

American family style is very personal to each of us. Its essence is revealed through our tastes and priorities—the very way that we live. When friends enter a home, they sense its personality. The feeling of the rooms, their aroma and character, the family's style of living—these elements make a house come alive with a sense of identity, a sense of energy, enthusiasm, and warmth, declaring "This is who we are; this is how we live."

My ideas of home and family are deeply rooted in what I knew growing up. I was raised by wonderful parents who loved their kids. When you grow up with parents who care about their children, it rubs off on you. My parents, my brothers and sister, their moods and tastes and projects gave scenery and shape to my life and inspired me to structure both my personal and professional lives around my family. Now that I have kids of my own, our family style is based on the same sense of involvement in each other's lives. It's a feeling that we share and pass on to the next generation.

We do not have an old tradition in America. We make it up as we go along. That is what gives American family style—*American style*—its vitality and its diversity. American style is born of individualism, people creating a style for themselves day to day, from things they feel good about. It is a style that defines you and inspires you to reach out and continue that evolution of who you are. I feel that it is just this spirit of invention that the Carters have captured in their homes—the same freshness that has inspired me in my work.

When I first read about the Carter home in Virginia, something touched me. I felt that they embodied a certain truly American quality—a great feeling of community, people who enjoy each other and spend time together, the table that expands quickly to accommodate friends and neighbors dropping by, the comfortable surroundings that welcome you home. I am delighted with this book, a recognition that American family style has, at last, come into its own.

Ralph Lauren

ACKNOWLEDGMENTS

This book is covered with family fingerprints—Carters, Christians, Bergs, Coateses, Thompsons, Donofrios, Nortons, Lightbourns, Dwyers, and Harlans—and those of all other family and friends who over the years have pitched in their love, creativity, and time by our sides in the kitchen, in the gardens, on ladders, and at the piano to help make Muskettoe Pointe Farm the crazy, joyous, blooming place—the home—it has become for all of us. Each of you, in your own way, has added to the spirit of that place and this book. Thank you.

Thank you, Mother and Father, for daring to have so many of us, for always being proud, for teaching us that what matters most in a home is love.

To my brothers and sisters, whose homes, husbands, wife, children, personal talents, and originality have breathed real life into our style and this book—thank you, Cary, Nell, Jimmie, Emily, Liza, Bernard, Christian, and Cleiland. Thank you, Hunter, David, John, Joni, Christopher, and, of course, Howard.

And to our children—Carter, Cary Hunter, Christian, David, Ed, Emily, Holly, John Christian, John Tyler, Mary Randolph, Sam, Tom, and Waller—who donned Halloween costumes, made the cookies, decorated the eggs, played the shepherds, and supplied the glue that keeps us all together—thank you.

Thank you, Ga-Ga, for all of this (all of us), and the love you've carried in your heart and around your wrist—all those golden circles and hearts engraved with all our initials, birthdates, children.

Thank you to my good friends—real photographers—who each in his or her own way encouraged me to take the pictures in this book: Brigitte Lacombe, Ariel Skelley, and Barbra Walz—and to Arthur Elgort and George Barkentin for the pictures taken almost a decade ago for *Mademoiselle,* a few of which appear in this book.

Thank you, Alexander Liberman, for your two decades of guidance at Condé Nast Publications, for always being a Carter family supporter, and for introducing me to Phyllis Starr Wilson, *Self*'s founding editor-in-chief, who always knew I could write, and to Val Weaver, her successor, who allowed me the freedom to actually do it, in good conscience, without leaving home.

Thank you, Hollis Diamandis, assistant, friend, and chief cheerleader; Sue Millar Perry, for your "yes-you-can" attitude; and Diane Smith, for your support and for introducing me to Steve Axelrod, my agent, who understood this book right away and led me in no time to just the right person—Michael Fragnito at Viking Penguin, who believed in *American Family Style* from our very first meeting and never stopped, and made this dream (it's true) a book. And to Barbara Williams, my editor—there are not enough pages (I told you already!) or words to express my awe at your sensitive scrutiny, advice, encouragement, grace, and elegance.

Marcia Weinberg (you've become a seventh sister!)—what a glorious scrapbook you've created. Thank you for the days, weeks, hours, those long, back-breaking meetings on the floor, for over a year out of your life.

Thank you, James Wharton, special friend, mentor, letter writer, word lover.

Thank you, Robert Carter Ball—Bobby—good friend and neighbor, who has always had a special vision of Muskettoe Pointe Farm—proof of which embellishes the endpapers of this book.

Thank you, Miriam Haynie, for *The Stronghold,* your history of the Northern Neck of Virginia that inspired the definition of our first Americans' family style in the introduction.

Thank you, Ralph Lauren, for your steadfast vision of America's family style and for sharing it with us in your foreword.

Thank you, "Echo Hill" gang—Harvey, Sharon, Luke, Lake, and Courtney—for always making your country getaway ours, and allowing pictures of those times in this book. Thank you, Columbia County friends: Kimmel and Richard, Barbara and Peter, Alice Reid of Reid's Antiques, Willard, the two Ripleys, Eddie, Marion, et al. Thank you, Outer Bankers, for sharing your sand-castle homes.

Thank you, Jann Johnson, for always inspiring; always sticking by me.

Thank you, Robin Bell Schafer, for early photographic collaborations—paper cutouts, paper-towel still lifes, terry towels, and ironstone soap dishes.

Thank you to my other mother and other Ga-Ga to Sam and Carter—Jean Landy Berg, and to Una Michaud, who has loved and cared for all of us as though we were her own.

And finally, to that family—founders of our style—who remain with us in spirit: Nell Christian, Liza Christian, Eleanor Christian, John Christian, and Bernard Carter—great-aunts, aunt, and two grandfathers—a whispered thanks.

AMERICAN
FAMILY STYLE

INTRODUCTION

It was in the wilderness of a new America, along the banks of creeks and rivers, behind the solidly built doors of cottages, huts, and cabins, around trestle and sawbuck tables draped with simple homespun and set with wooden bowls and pewter, that the first American families gave thanks for their food, homes, and new sense of freedom. Their family style was based on teamwork and sharing. Each family member played some part in its daily survival—from clearing the land to setting the table. Neighbors pitched in to help dig a well, raise a barn, toast the birth of a child, a good harvest, a wedding, Christmas, and—one day—their independence. These families' strong individualism, faith, perseverance, resourcefulness, good sense, and sense of humor are the qualities that have inspired this book.

American family style is an adventure shared by all American families, large or small. It's finding real-life comforts in everyday objects, spontaneous solutions to every-day problems. It's working things out with what's at hand to add the from-the-heart details that make a house a home and guests feel like family. It's essentially democratic, a style that leaves room for everybody at any age or stage of life to find his or her own form of expression. It's a style moored in the past yet committed to the future—the traditions, customs, and rituals that new generations carry with them to start homes of their own. It's a style that has nothing to do with specific periods of furniture or types of food yet has everything to do with how they're presented. It's as personal as a thumbprint.

In the pages that follow you will join three generations of one American family as they live their own family style throughout the seasons. But there are as many American family styles as there are American families. This book only begins to explore the endless possibilities. The rest is left up to the vital imaginations of its readers—American families, masters of ingenuity.

The house had always been there. We had driven past it a thousand times on the way to River Barn, our summer house—later home—on the Rappahannock River in Virginia's Tidewater region. Mother would sometimes point to the ancient horse and buggy sending up little clouds of dust as its driver trotted it down the tree-arched lane that led from the house to the blacktop road known as Pigtail Alley. That blacktop surface was the driver's borderline. He'd go no farther, just rein in the horse, turn the buggy around, and continue back to the house, where his sister, Gertrude Lawson (Miss Gertie to all who knew her), waited supper. Father had told us Miss Gertie's husband's family had once owned all the land along our road and much of the surrounding area. They had built Muskettoe Pointe Farm in the late seventeenth century (in 1680, according to one Lawson family historian) and named it after an Indian word, *muskettoe,* pronounced "mosquito" but meaning "a high, grassy plain." After a while the buggy stopped coming and we heard Miss Gertie had died. The house and land were put up for sale and we continued past it, while families of raccoons and cats settled in comfortably upstairs and down, wind and rain swept through open windows and doors, and honeysuckle vines quickly crept over the shingled exterior, transforming it into a seventeenth-century version of Sleeping Beauty's castle.

Left: *Our Sleeping Beauty's castle—Muskettoe Pointe Farm—the way we found it almost thirty years ago.* Above: *A restaining of the exterior by family and friends became a weekend project several years back.* Right: *A glimpse of the house almost twenty-five years later through a stalwart guardian of hundreds of years—a paper mulberry tree. The house has grown, along with the family, to include two new additions, to the left of the original, and at least two chimneys.*

Left: *A family portrait from 1972, almost ten years after our family project had begun.* Below right: *Our new view of the Rappahannock.* Opposite, top: *Two of the restored dependencies.* Opposite, bottom: *A birdhouse replica of Muskettoe Pointe Farm—a gift from our carpenters.*

We were a large family—seven girls, two boys ("come-heres," so called because we came from someplace else), from Richmond, birthplace of our parents and all of us—when we decided to make our summer house, River Barn, our year-round home. The night it burned, three years later, I was sixteen, the oldest. The youngest was not quite one. My parents were younger than I am now. We crawled down the narrow staircase, bent low, clutching one another in a frightened train, until we stood outside counting our number over and over. We had made it, all of us, even our Saint Bernard, who later went back in (missing Father, we think, who had left the scene for a moment) and was lost. Our family style began that night.

For a year we were nomads, celebrating Christmas, the Fourth of July, birthdays, and anniversaries in make-believe homes. We had decided not to rebuild River Barn but to start over in a house on a new piece of land, down a different road, looking out on another part of the river. An architect had already drawn up the plans when one day Mom and Dad drove back down our old road and turned up the lane where that horse and buggy had long since trotted to look at the fifteen acres that were up for sale. The little ruined house halfway in was almost an after-thought. Father chopped his way to the front door and pulled Mother up into a wide entrance hall littered with the carnage of an old house unloved and unlived-in for al-most ten years—fallen plaster, broken glass, rampant vines, and the calling cards of all the four-legged, furry transients that had long since abandoned it. At the other end of the hall lay another set of doors, which opened onto a stretch of land, a bluff, a beach, the Rappahannock, and, beyond it, the mouth of the Chesapeake Bay. They thought then that maybe this was the place (so close to where we had lived before) to begin again. We children,

after all, might be comforted to take the same school bus around those familiar turns, to swim and crab in the same waters we had for summers and summers. They put away the plans for the new house, put the land up for sale, and started a family project to restore this funny old tilty farm-house and fifteen acres that, somewhere along the way, re-stored us.

No architect was hired—"Maybe that was a mistake," says Mother with a laugh. We relied just on family and very good friends, which meant weekends and weekdays after school and work spent hacking through the honeysuckle and tangled growth that had enveloped the house in a brambled cocoon. The inside work crew looked like a gang of bandits, with red and blue bandannas tied around their faces to protect them (somewhat) from the storms of plaster dust flying up everywhere. One wallpaper peeler swears she uncovered thirty-two layers on an upstairs bed-room wall; another, attacking a pile of debris like a hungry archaeologist, gave out a blood-curdling shriek as her search was rewarded with the not-quite-fossilized remains of an unfortunate cat family.

You can follow our family project by turning to the end-paper map of Muskettoe Pointe Farm, created for us with love by our good friend Robert Carter Ball—Bobby. In real life, the fifteen acres form a long, skinny rectangle that runs from the entrance gate straight to the river. Artistic license has prevailed somewhat, so that what should be the top half of the map is actually flopped over to the

and Mother would walk out in the field and try to visualize the pitch of the roof—pull on it, push at it—until they got it the way they wanted. Eventually, local carpenters, plasterers, and bricklayers—artisans, many of whom had helped us make River Barn habitable—returned. Before they departed, almost a year later, we had finished the new wing, two new chimneys, and five fireplaces. We had restored three dependencies—the early name given to a little outbuilding that a main house depended on: ours, lined up to the left of the house, north of the guest quarters, were a pointed-roof smokehouse, a storage house, and a well house. Eventually, they were all connected by old brick footpaths that wandered from door to door and out to the gardens. We also built a children's playhouse, fenced in behind the dependencies, and a barn. The barn, designed by Father, is a composite of all the favorite barn features he and Mother had savored on trips up and down the Eastern seaboard—clipped gable, arched doorways, a hayloft dormer, overhanging roof rafters, and a wooden shake roof. Last, but not least, we finished the beach house—the slightly scorched sole surviving structure of our old River Barn (find it at the bottom of the right-hand page, with a dock extending out from it).

right-hand page. After you enter the farm through either gate at the bottom of the left-hand page, greeted by all the family and our pets, you should head up the road (waving to Ga-Ga and Sister, Father's mother and sister visiting from Richmond, then to Scrabble, our horse) past the barn in the upper right-hand corner. In real life, you would go straight ahead through the picket-fence entrance gate at the top of the right-hand page. Follow the path past the lineup of dependencies (left), and face the house with the river to your back. It is divided into three distinct sections. The tallest of the three, to the far left, is the seventeenth-century original where we began our cleanup operation. This original house contained no inside bathrooms. There was a small kitchen and a dining-room addition tacked onto the back about seventy years ago, which was severed by us immediately and dragged to its present location just left of the house (follow the path), where it now shelters guests and our growing families. The new wing, to the right, an obvious necessity, indented a little from the original structure, gave us the kind of eat-in/live-in kitchen a large family needs. Above it, there was a bedroom for Mother and Father, with a big porch off it, under which our springtime swallows nest. We also squeezed in three little bathrooms—two upstairs and one, "the pee-wee," in an old closet in the library.

It had been fall when we started all this. It was spring—Easter weekend, the following year—when we moved in. The seams that separate the centuries—seventeenth to twentieth—were practically invisible. The third and final wing of the house, closest to the herb garden and sporting two chimneys, was added in time for Christmas—three years later.

When this wing was added, Father devised a way of planking off everything with two-by-fours and putting up a dummy to make sure we had the right proportions. He

The following spring, a vegetable garden inspired by Mount Vernon's was planted outside the new kitchen's windows (in the map's upper right-hand corner, between the two picket fences). A year or two later, those vegetables were replanted closer to the river (where the birdhouse stands on the map) and replaced by a variety of herbs, which began to appear mashed in our butter, in crocks as decorations, and entwined in grapevine wreaths—our new family imprimatur. Mother had resisted

Right: *Four Carter weddings have taken place at Muskettoe Pointe Farm. The first two were celebrated under a wisteria arbor close to the house. The site of the last two was the bank in front of the log cabin overlooking the Rappahannock. The wedding processions would start at the house—see Liza on Father's arm, below—and meet at the edge of this peaceful view. The locust trees stand like swaying witnesses.*

a flower garden for years, but soon thereafter Father designed a formal pair (inspired by English prototypes) and laid them out right off the back of the house (as you can see on the map), divided by a brick footpath that led from the original wing's back door straight toward the river. The beds of planted periwinkle, daffodils, and tulips were protected by chubby borders of English boxbushes, the first of some three hundred to dot our landscape over the years. The biggest threat was not footloose children but our Saint Bernards (new ones since the fire) and their puppies, who would forever flop their huge furry bodies into those beds as if they were theirs.

The last real structure built at Muskettoe Pointe Farm was started our tenth summer there—a log cabin (in the lower right-hand corner of the right-hand page) built of trapstakes, young pine trees used by local fishermen to hold up their nets. It was built near the edge of the riverbank to take advantage of the view and the summertime breezes. Mostly it's used as a backdrop for holiday picnics, a silvery retreat from the main house's chaos, a great place

to store extraneous furniture, and a drying room for fields of just-picked yarrow—and twice it was the site of Carter daughters' weddings.

It will be twenty-five years this spring—Easter weekend—since Muskettoe Pointe Farm welcomed us home. I was seventeen, a senior in high school, named Mary Randolph after Mother (who was always called Pat, as I was called Tippy); Cary Christian, fifteen, was the first of four of us to receive Mother's maiden name as her middle one; Nell Christian, the third sister, had just become a teenager; James Northam, Jr.—Jimmie (the first son, named after Father)—was twelve; Emily Everett, ten, named after Ga-Ga (as Sister was), made the third generation of E.E.C.s; Liza Christian was eight; Bernard Pitzer was six; Anne Christian, called Christian, was three; and Cleiland Donnan was two. A lot has happened since then—much more than gardens planted, furniture collected, a log cabin finished. Mother and Father started their own real-estate business on the main street of the little town that soon became familiar territory—the post office and the combination of turns to

Left: *The Carter family, summer of 1987: standing left to right are Emily Carter holding daughter Emily Donofrio, Cary Carter Coates holding an upside-down John Christian Donofrio also held by Howard Berg, Mary Randolph Carter Berg, Nell Carter Thompson holding Cary Hunter Thompson, Jimmie Carter, Holly Coates, Father and Mother, John Norton, Liza Carter Norton holding Mary Randolph Norton, Christian Thompson, Hunter Thompson, Cleiland Carter, Christian Carter Lightbourn, Christopher Lightbourn, and Bernard and Joni Johnston Carter. Seated left to right are David Donofrio and son David, Carter Berg, Sam Berg, and bandanna-clad dog Jude. Missing are Tom Coates, Ed and Waller Thompson, and an unborn John Tyler Norton.*

the left and the right that granted children used to having their mail delivered wondrous access to the mysterious envelopes behind box number 7; the brick grocery store where everybody knew us; the hardware store with one narrow aisle that snaked its way through merchandise twelve feet high through two adjoining buildings—where Cary got lost once; the movie theater where the last movie shown was *The Ten Commandments*; the drugstore with those twirling racks of comic books; and, around the corner, behind Dad and Mom's office, the Texaco station known to us simply as Berry's (the owner's first name), our after-school headquarters for bottles of Coke and orange Tru-ades pulled from the freezing-cold water of old-fashioned coolers, cellophaned packages of peanut-butter Nabs, Mary Janes, Squirrels, see-through bags of candy corn, peppermint patties, and fistfuls of Dubble Bubble— all of which Berry would start to add up on the back of a paper bag until a car rolled over the rubber hose next to the gas pumps, setting off a ring that would interrupt his calculations and precipitate our departure.

Every year there were apples to bob for, piles of leaves to jump in, snow to wish for, a Christmas tree to decorate, Easter eggs to dye, gardens to weed, crabs to catch, stinging nettles to watch out for, and Happy Birthdays to sing over and over. Six years after our arrival, we celebrated our first family wedding under an open trapstake "tabernacle" built for the occasion and entwined with wisteria. After seven marriages and eighteen years, the grandchild count—six girls and seven boys—is pretty modest, considering the precedent.

Three of us have made our homes in New York City— one with an outpost in the mountains. Three more are closer to home, in Richmond. Emily and David are just finishing a home a stone's throw from the entrance at Muskettoe Pointe; a few miles away, Jimmie has just moved into a sparkling white and glass-windowed retreat, cuddled by pines and a nearby creek; and Christian and Christopher are celebrating their third year in Nassau by moving into an old stone dream house on a hill high above another bay.

Afriend once described Muskettoe Pointe Farm as the mothership. She imagined it floating way above the earth with nine little satellites (our new homes and families) whirling around it, all connected by long strings of lavender. Several times a year, the mothership gongs out a signal and we pull ourselves home by our herbal umbilical cords to celebrate Christmas, spring's arrival, or an old-fashioned Fourth of July picnic on the river. She imagined that, if while we were otherwise engaged she crept unannounced through our satellite homes (as Goldilocks did through the house of the three bears), she would find rooms, chairs, beds, and porridge not so very different from those of the mothership that guides us along. She was right, of course. Our homes—apartments in Manhattan, old houses in Richmond—have family fingerprints all over them. We've each taken little or big gobs of our family's style (Jimmie calls it "family stew") with us. In some cases, it's funny old furniture, family disguises, an herb garden tucked in a city windowbox, or the sweet home smell of lavender wafting everywhere.

Father once said that Muskettoe Pointe was "just a place that people built." He was right. Like any home, it was created by all kinds of friends and family—come-heres and born-heres, weeders, growers, grocery shoppers, cooks, bakers, dishwashers, music makers, dancers, singers, storytellers, poets, rabble-rousers, wreath makers, harvesters, barn raisers, suitors, savers, lovers, turkey carvers, Christmas-tree finders, toast givers, list makers, sweepers, candle lighters, table setters, magicians, polishers, baby-sitters, cheerleaders, artists, hand holders, bartenders, welcomers, haulers, scrapers, peelers, mood setters, arrangers, sorters, scrubbers, washers, dryers, camouflagers, huggers, passers, discoverers.

Left: *Spring of 1977 celebrated by a train of sisters romping through the daisies.*

FALL

FALL

ENTRANCES

The real welcome to Muskettoe Pointe Farm begins with the click of the signal arm as you enter the leafy tunnel, left, that takes you along a weathered fence where family pets—Norfolk, Suffolk, and Hampshire sheep, two horses named Blue Tail and Scrabble, and a burro dubbed Soul Sister—used to roam. Cedars, bayberries, and hollies freckled with color hint at what's to come: lots of crunchy castles across our lawns, apple picking, Halloween spirits, football games, and the smell of turkey from our ovens.

Above: A fall joyride on the tailgate of "Jim-Pa's" truck (my father's nickname, given him by his thirteen grandchildren).

There are five entrances to Muskettoe Pointe Farm, but it's the side door (above) off the kitchen that welcomes most. A covered stoop offers entrants a sheltered pause as they scuff their muddied shoes over some Carter wisdom (below). An old lantern hung from a peg lights the way at night, while an abandoned football and an antique pitchfork stand in for more usual signs of life: Igloo coolers, bags of ice, cartons of "red eye"*—icebox overflow now out of sight.

*My brother-in-law David's name for Coke. When he was a child, in lieu of a cocktail, a cousin would give him a Coke with a cherry in it—"it would float to the surface like a red eye."

Right: *John Christian, age three, makes an entrance through the kitchen door.*

A well-seasoned door: aged pine flavored with a wreath of sage from the kitchenside herb garden.

An anchor-eye door hasp on a dependency door. Dad's collection of old locks adorns every portal at Muskettoe Pointe.

A bushy gate of ten-foot yews tickles passersby as they travel through to the double front doors, once red, now black.

A cloverhead sliding gate hasp, attached for years to Muskettoe Pointe's herb-garden gate, is rarely locked.

17

Left: *"Knock, Knock." "Who's there?" It's a foxy brass door knocker on the guest-house door. The salt air has oxidized his lines and furrows a greeny blue, and the screen door has smoothed the tip of his too-pointy nose.*

Far left: *Inside the front door, a corner of cudgels, canes, shillelaghs, and umbrellas sprout like strange stalks from a brown pottery measure. Not an old family collection, but an instant one—auction loot. Mom plopped them in that pot with the price tags on and never took them off.*

Above: *The real treasure of the front hall is not the Queen Anne armchair losing a bit of its bottom, or the rather stern pair of ancestral portraits, or the fine oaken English blanket chest, or the primitive pewter charger on top—but a secret trapdoor beneath chair and chest hauled open by a rope swag, which reveals steps to a mysterious cellar room below. The trapdoor was added after the original outside entrance to the cellar was closed up.*

Inside a side door, a narrow twist of stairs is warmed by old panel-
ing and Virginia maps. The room at the top (far right), over the
kitchen and through the hall, is Mom and Dad's. It's part of the not-
so-loneliness-proof quarters they created for themselves after we had
left to make our own. The bedroom's lit with lots of sun, a fireplace
at night, and a bedside lamp that spells PAT.

Along the preceding hallway, lined with hodgepodge doors, are
tucked a cozy bathroom with a mustard-painted pedestal tub, two
bookshelves (one each on the right and left of the hall just before the
bedroom door) filled with Mom's gardening favorites and C. P.
Snows, a shallow closet for skinny shirts and narrow shoes, and pretty
boards all in a row.

Dependencies are the smaller outer buildings a main house depends on, like this little shingled storage house, formerly the cellar entrance to Muskettoe Pointe Farm.

The last step down from Muskettoe Pointe's side-entrance stoop is a diagonally slatted wooden mat for sandy shoes.

For twenty years this dovecote's not seen a feather. Because it's built into the back of the well-house wall, it could be that the pump's too noisy.

The gate to the three-mile-wide river at the back of the house was made by Bernard of hand-split white-oak pickets. Grapevine wreaths crown one post.

A welcome wreath wound from wisteria vines in Cary's Richmond backyard was decorated one Christmas with a shiny heart and a fuzzy bird.

A second wreath, on our upstate New York farmhouse door, shelters a wrinkled walnut couple from the chilly breezes of fall.

A one-inch wooden spotted creature, found on a trek in Nepal, now stalks arriving guests from a Victorian oak newel facing Cary's front door.

Nell and Hunter swapped country for city, shingles for stone. Their home in Richmond has European accents—French lace doves at the window and an English cast-cement whippet on his throne—but the Muskettoe Pointe Farm grapevine wreath is the family imprimatur: no matter how remote or how unusual, here's another Carter home.

This is our get-away-from-the-city house (the home of the walnut couple a page back), far from Virginia, in view of the Catskill Mountains. Fall accelerates quickly here. Before you know it, the leaves are down. The children love to tell the story about our first fall there, when they raked up piles of leaves and I made them scatter them all back because I love the way they cover the ground like a richly patterned kilim. Making an entrance, above, is our younger son, Sam. He seems in step with the goose that guards our door and the black-and-white pig leading from the far window, left. Whenever we're home we fly our flag, emblazoned with the colonists' cry "Dont Tread on Me." I wonder if our neighbors have taken offense.

Right: *At the end of the day the goose comes in (and so do leaves) to rest in the entrance hall and contemplate an oval of flowers. The boys pile their mitts and balls, beside knobbly walking sticks, in an umbrella stand that's built of what look like toy Lincoln Logs.*

We leave this wicker creel behind
When we're fishing for fish or flea-market finds.
If you stop by and we're not in
Leave us a note—or maybe a fin.

It may be bad poetry, but it's not a bad idea, our creel on the front door (see full view, left). We've yet to find a message or any kind of fin inside, but we like the way it looks on the door.

A big lesson from home was to make sure guests felt welcome and warmed the minute they walked through the front door. In an entranceway (below) big enough only for a hug, that's a challenge to do. The welcoming party on the wall, housed in a tri-level pine shelf, is always changing—a wooden Saint Nick with barrel in tow, a walnut couple dressed for town, and sepia homespun women lined up in a pose. On the yellow table stenciled with flowers, below it, skinny enough to just escape being banged by the opening door, there's always a pitcher or a pot of something green and emptied pocket change or keys. Standing by are favorite English souvenirs—a pair of rubber gardening boots and, on the wall above them, a greeting card in a dime-store frame. The door to the left leads to the fireplace room, where an apple-wood fire warms our welcomes from early fall to early June.

WILDLIFE

Left: *A string of trout scooped out of a shop in up-state New York, near freshwater streams. One wonders if the artist of this primitive oil ever really fished!*

Within our homes lurk grizzly bears, antlered deer, horned owls, ducks, geese, mantel trophies, and strings of fish. Mind where you sit or step or even gaze—they could surprise you—but other than that they're really harmless. Imaginary wildlife preserved in paint or carved from wood and stone, they're tributes to the outdoor sporting life that gives a home (city or country) some hunting-lodge soul.

Preceding illustration: *A marsh in Virginia is the site of Silk Sheets, Hunter and friends' rustic retreat. There's a wood-burning stove inside for warmth, a grill outside for fish, bunk beds, indoor plumbing, and, as Hunter says, "It's unique."*

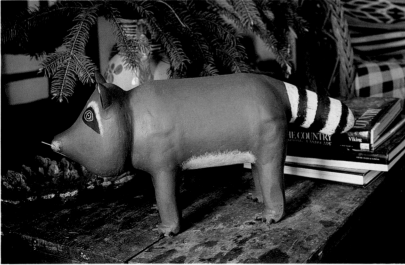

Far left: *Last year's most original Christmas gift, from Emily to How-ard—a plastic predator used in Virginia to keep gulls off docks and crows out of cherry trees. In our house in the country we hope it scares mice.*

Above: *Looking as though he had just emerged from the mountain-ous terrain framed behind him, this toy grizzly stands his ground on a wobbly twig table next to a sturdy hickory Adirondack chair.*

Left: *A toothpick-whiskered "Rocky Raccoon," this wood-and-paint whimsy by the Santa Fe artist David Alvarez traveled all the way to its coffee-table home in New York State, plied with succulent evergreen boughs and a tasty pile of books.*

W elcome to the "Teddy Roosevelt room" in our upstate New York retreat. Everything in it is dedicated to the outdoors. We'll start our tour in the doorway, above.

Above: *Across the hall there's a lift-top commode. On top—a basket of papier-mâché fruit and a cup of tea . . . sorry, it's cold! Above it are Hudson Valley landscapes in oil and next to it a rickety chair of the Adirondack style. The straw hat on the wall hides a fixture the owners don't like and the hooked checkerboard rug is a fragile delight.*

Middle left: *Stepping into the room, we'll move to the right, where a red hickory rocker and its straight-legged mate share a shaky twig table and the shade of a ficus. Its leaves brush the canvas of some strange-looking deer found in North Carolina and transported here.*

Top: *On the flip-top table opened into a bar resides a trio of deer: to the left, mighty antlers of papier-mâché; between the spruce and the cedar, a second appears in relief from a plaster forest; and above, the same scene in oil. For a closer look, see the picture below, middle right. The hurricane shades there rest in dollbaby tubs; the long, thin twigs are cinnamon sticks.*

Bottom left: *A bird's-nest cache for spicy sticks and a pinecone spine.* Bottom right: *a pair of handmade songbirds singing for their supper.*

Left: *A step past the bar (lit by a homemade jug lamp) stands a spindle-back, light-hickory chair. Between it and the blanket-covered captain's chair is an altar to wild-life—a muddy-red table topped with decoys by the North Carolina wood-carver Charles Reber, souvenirs from Alaska—an ashtray, a scented pillow, and a book, a proud pair of bookend profiles, and a doll's patchwork coverlet under it all. Enshrined above—three "3-D" scenes from nature, by unsung artists from upstate New York, and "the one that didn't get away" decorated with a live cherry branch.*

Far left: *Across the room there's a ship's card table with a red weighted base and three splint-bottomed Adirondack chairs. The table is covered with an American Indian blanket and holds an unusual lamp (see close-up, bottom right), begged away from the owner's mother and detested by her husband: "Whenever I go to turn on that light I get stuck by metal pine needles and a bird that bites!" A green ceramic peacock cigarette holder and ashtrays were gifts to the collection from a nonsmoking friend. The bunches of grapes framed on the wall are hand-colored pages from a nurseryman's log. The frames, of the five-and-ten-cent-store variety, were painted a deep greenish blue. The sewing-machined curtains, of tartan flannel, are the same hue. And last but not least, at the end of our tour, in the shadowy left corner, we direct your attention to an outdoor treasure brought indoors. It's the finest example of a birdhouse-on-pole, a Mother's Day endowment from a year or two ago. The tiny turkey in the close-up, top right, was a late-fall acquisition; the cherry-laden branch, a "Home, Sweet Home" addition.*

FALL

PICKINGS

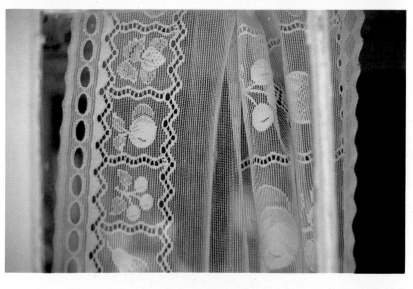

As children, we never picked apples. In our part of Virginia the colonists planted mulberry trees to feed and house silkworms for a fledgling silk industry. Unfortunately, however, at Muskettoe Pointe Farm they planted paper mulberries—the wrong kind for silkworms. Only the trees survived. Our family's only apple history is candied apples at the firemen's carnival, apple butter out of the jar, bobbing for apples at Halloween parties, fried apples for breakfast—and no apple pies. But today, our children pick bushels of apples, Liza bakes oodles of apple pies, one of us has found a house in an orchard, and there's an apple tree blooming at Muskettoe Pointe Farm.

Top: *On a country kitchen windowsill, a farmhouse miniature by a ten-year-old and wax replicas of an apple, two pears, and a pepper.*

Middle: *On a sideboard at Nell's, a birchbark box of ornamental cabbage nestled in Spanish moss and tucked with Emily's bouquets of lavender. Lined up in front are four shiny wooden apples and a flowery tile.*

Bottom: *Apples, pears, peaches, berries—gauzey fruit by the yard hanging in our orchard house's sun-room window.*

Right: *Orchard tender: a bushel basket of just-picked Macouns.*

Preceding illustration: *What to do with those inedible apples? Throw a garden party for the birds! Ours, an impromptu affair in our backyard orchard, featured rustic spiraled furniture and overripe apple hors d'oeuvres.*

At left, at work in Muskettoe Pointe's kitchen, one disheveled lock hanging down, is Liza, with a big fall breakfast under way and well in hand. The results, at right, include (from front of the table to back) Virginia apples, a pewter humidor of sugar, indestructible pewter plates, a pitcher of orange juice, herbs (in a colander) for color and flavor, a bowl of fried apples—the favored Carter apple preparation (recipe below)—bacon and sausage, mugs of forks and knives, loaves of bread, spoon bread, homemade herb butter, and apple jelly.

HOWARD'S PLUM APPLESAUCE

An apple memory from Howard's childhood in Fall River, Massachusetts.

10 apples (Macoun or McIntosh), peeled, cored, and cut into quarters
8 damsons or black plums
¹/₂ cup water
¹/₂ cup light brown sugar
¹/₂ teaspoon cinnamon
¹/₈ teaspoon nutmeg

Simmer apples and plums with water in a heavy saucepan, covered, 20–25 minutes. Stir occasionally and add water if necessary to keep fruit from scorching. Add remaining ingredients and stir 3 minutes. Drain excess water. Cover and refrigerate.
Makes 6 cups.

EASY APPLES

Fried apples are a year-round tradition for our Sunday morning breakfasts. Though we've done them from scratch, especially during fall when we can buy apples by the bushel, we usually take the easy way out by substituting apple pie filling.

1 cup light brown sugar
¹/₂ stick butter
2 cans apple pie filling
1 tablespoon lemon juice
¹/₂ teaspoon nutmeg

Melt sugar with butter in a frying pan, then add pie filling and seasonings. Simmer, uncovered, about 10 minutes.
Serves eight.

LIZA'S PIECRUST

Mother has always been the great cook of the family, but Liza is *the* baker. It's not something that happened overnight. She thinks she started at ten and admits to plenty of flops. "And lots of chaos in the kitchen—flour flying, pots stacked up—but," insists a brother-in-law/cook mate, "the results are always worth it." Below, Liza's apple pie "family" of five.

3 cups all-purpose flour, sifted
3 tablespoons sugar
1/2 teaspoon salt
1/2 cup cold butter
2/3 cup shortening
5–6 tablespoons ice water

In a bowl sift together flour, sugar, and salt. With a pastry blender (or with two knives used like scissors), cut butter and shortening into the dry ingredients until pea-sized dough balls form. Sprinkle ice water 1 tablespoon at a time over different parts of the mixture, tossing quickly with a fork until dough sticks together. (The secret of a light, flaky crust is to work as quickly as possible.) Lightly form dough into a ball. Wrap in plastic and refrigerate 1 hour.

Cut dough into two balls. Put one ball on floured surface and knead four times, then flatten slightly. Roll out with a rolling pin in all directions, forming a circle 1/8-inch thick. Fold piecrust in half or wrap gently around the rolling pin to place crust in bottom of a pie pan.

Fill and bake according to directions below.

Makes one 9-inch double crust or two 9-inch single crusts.

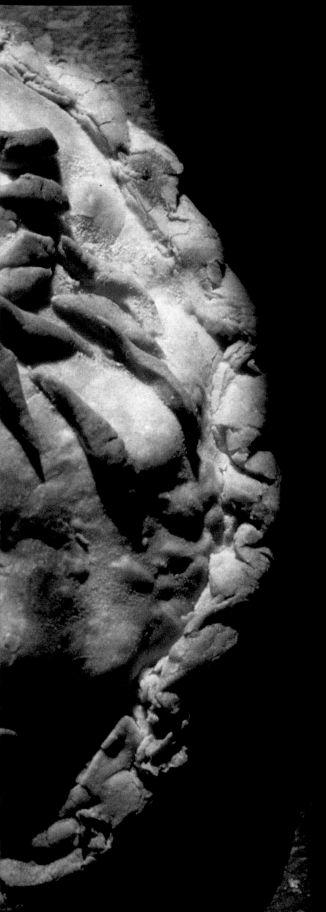

Above: *Homemade piecrust awaiting its cargo of apple pie filling. The finished product, left, with an engraved-in-crust family tree, is ready to be eaten.*

FAMILY APPLE PIE

5–6 apples (Granny Smiths are Liza's choice), peeled,
    cored, and sliced
$1/2$ cup dark raisins
1 tablespoon lemon juice
2 teaspoons vanilla extract
$1/2$ cup light brown sugar
$1/4$ cup granulated sugar
1 teaspoon cinnamon
$1/2$ teaspoon nutmeg
$1/2$ teaspoon mace
1 tablespoon flour
2 tablespoons butter
1 9-inch piecrust, store-bought or homemade (see
    above)

Toss apples and raisins with lemon juice. Sprinkle vanilla extract 1 teaspoon at a time over fruit and toss after each sprinkling. Mix together remaining ingredients, except butter, and toss with fruit. Pour apple mixture into piecrust. Dot apples with thin slices of butter. Top with piecrust and crimp bottom and top crusts together. Make slits in top crust so steam can escape during baking. Bake in a preheated 350-degree oven 45–50 minutes, until golden brown.
Serves eight to ten.

FALL

DISGUISES

On Halloween we took old sheets
And cut out holes so the kids could peek.
John Christian refused to put his on.
David, age five, said, "Mine's too long."
Emily, age two, just cried and cried,
And Christian, age nine, stood thoughtfully by.

We wanted to prevent any trick-or-treat flops
So we decided to add a surprise to our stops.
It lay at the end of a very long lane;
It was dusk by the time we took down the chain.

Preceding illustration: *Just weeks before it was razed to the ground, an abandoned (haunted!) farmhouse with Victorian touches made the perfect first stop on a ghostly trio's Halloween rounds.*

The doors were wide open, nobody about;
The sign on the porch read "No trespassing. Keep out."
Without a thought we tiptoed in;
The house, you see, was owned by a friend.

The children, by now, getting into the mood,
Floated and shrieked and let loose loud boos!
They climbed from the top to the bottom of the house
And kept their eyes peeled for a raccoon or a mouse.

As the sun sank behind the Great Wicomico River,
We decided it was time to get ourselves hither.
Back in the car, the children sat silent—
Being a ghost was a "wearing" assignment!

Disguises have always been a family thing. Not just at Halloween, turning children into ghosts, but all year long, continually dabbling to make things seem what they're not. Worn-out upholstery gets magic coverlets, a refrigerator door exhibits a new-wave poster, a decoupage screen masks insurmountable clutter. "Guests in the driveway! Turn off the lights—light up the candles! Hide the toys inside the basket . . . throw some flowers in front of that light switch. Turn up the music! Run for cover!" Five family-style lessons in the art of illusion.

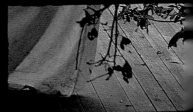

Sheets costume ghostly pretenders, right, as well as casement windows, above left, twelve stories up. Found in the country and brought to the city, they camouflage an ungraceful air conditioner while softening the view with lineny folds and billows. The chaise longue in shadow, bottom left, changes for warmer weather, bottom right, into crisp white slipcovers gauzed over with a huge antique tablecloth, embroidered pillows, and works by Matisse and Georgia O'Keeffe.

Right: *A blithe spirit clad in jeans and a queen-size cotton sheet awaits a trick or a treat outside the silent doorway of the "haunted house" up the lane.*

"Lay me in a cushioned chair;
Carry me, ye four,
With cushions here and cushions there,
To see the world once more."

An eloquent refrain borrowed from "The Ballad of the Foxhunter" by William Butler Yeats and spoken by the make-believe Martian, above left, not unlike a misplaced E.T., who rests in an eighteenth-century comb-back Windsor armchair in the living room of Muskettoe Pointe Farm. The cushioned chair, above, awaits him in a sunny corner of his earthling grandparents' bedroom upstairs. It's a dandified affair upholstered with satiny stripes and fringe all over. The back was pretty badly worn (as were the arms!), so Grandmother flung a rudimentary patchwork quilt over it—one of those totally mismatched marriages that sometimes works.

This is Howard's chair. For years he's been yearning for something comfortable to sit in. Finally, I found it. Not a Chippendale wing, but a knockoff from the twenties or thirties with a cherry frame and upholstered with a wonderfully faded, earthy linen fabric—the real reason I bought it. A little worse for wear—the fabric and the falling-out bottom—but I promised I'd have it repaired and recovered. In the interim, it's "togaed" with an old stripe-and-paisley spread that reminds me of something an eccentric English writer might wrap up in while working in her study. To date, nothing's changed, except the owl that's taken over.

A plain but good-hearted armchair got the Pygmalion treatment under Liza's tutelage. The first stage consisted of simple tattersall upholstery in Liza's first apartment's living room. After marriage and a move to a larger space, the chair moved too—into the bedroom. Surrounded by romantic linen and lace, the chair took on an air of stodginess. A search through the stalls of a city flea market turned up the very garb that was needed—a one-of-a-kind drapery blooming with feathery ferns, lilacs, and elephant ears. But Liza found more. An antique silk fringed shawl was draped over one tattersalled shoulder. The plain-Jane chair now lives happily ever after.

Above: *Personal camouflage: a big black beret and a star-studded fan.*

Left: *An exotic backdrop for Chippendale chairs and artificial fruit—Liza calls it "the scream"—a twelve-foot, three-panel, hand-painted wonder "that divides or hides, depending on our need."*

Below: *A child's Victorian screen decoupaged with myriad turn-of-the-century magazine illustrations. While ownership is debated, it shields cornered clutter in the guest-house bedroom.*

FALL

Secret Gardens

Left: *A cutting basket of dried long-stemmed red rose-buds mixed with stat-ice dropped next to a rose-wreathed needlepoint pillow and a backup batch made from ragtag quilt scraps.*

Above: *Love's tokens—rosebuds from romantic bouquets—make a garden in a pewter bowl. It thrives on a sun-dappled pine table bordered by another passion—majolica plates.*

Far right: *Someone (not me) lovingly filled this oval frame with a chalice of roses, jonquils, blue knotweed, and wildflowers.*

Right: *Like real-life flowers and fruit, this painted arrangement and plate full of grapes are passed from room to room. Today they mingle with needlepoint flowers on a bench in the library. Tomorrow?*

Preceding illustration: *In the guest house at Muskettoe Pointe Farm, an old print of pansies dangles from an ivy-entwined wire.*

All of us are entitled to a "bit of earth"—Mary Lennox's humble request in *The Secret Garden*. But when we can't have even this little bit—an apartment is twelve stories up, for example, or the season is uncooperative—we need gardens that will bloom from surprise places inside our homes: from paintings, plates, or the intricate stitches of a crocheted pillow. Some gardens are fragrant, others are dried. When we were children, our secret gardens were lodged in storybooks and in the hollow of a tree at Mother's uncle's farm in Virginia. One summer that we stayed there, we made a miniature "fairy garden" and a tiny "fairy village." At night we would stare out our bedroom window straining to see that distant tree and imagined we saw dancing lights and heard the sound of tiny tinkling chimes, harps, and violins.

Every visit home (to Muskettoe Pointe Farm) reveals some new delight. A couple of Christmases ago it was the sage and rosebud standard, right, not grown but created (yes, faked) by our own masterful garden sorcerer—Emily. Knowing the sore limitations of my sorry green thumb and envisioning how splendid (and maintenance-free) this herbal edifice would look in our home, I grabbed—but was told "hands off" by Em, who explained it was already spoken for. So how did I come by it (since I obviously did)? Two days later, on Christmas morn, it was under the tree with a big LOVE FROM EMILY card and was even repotted in a worthy spatterware bucket. It now stands alone on a three-legged throne, an old English cricket table, next to a sofa of needlepoint pillows, a full wall of samplers, and a little heart mirror. I recently discovered what it always reminded me of—those rose-covered standards in *Alice in Wonderland,* near which Alice played croquet with the Queen.

The same Christmas that I got my sage and rosebud standard Nell got her miniature mop-headed pair, above. According to Emily, the creator and giver, the yellow-tinged herb we've been poking fun at (apologies extended) is lemon verbena. Since there's no leakage threat (dried standards aren't watered), Nell gave them honored spots on top of her prized mahogany sideboard. Above them, between the two maple mirrors, is Christian's wedding bouquet of herbs. (For a closer look, see page 168.) The other hinted-at gardens come from the quartet of landscapes—a pair on either side of the mirrors. And, back on the sideboard, a pair of blue-and-white platters and matching soup bowls bloom with delicate rose borders.

In our New York City apartment, a lone ficus tree catches its daily dose of southern light. For thirteen years, it's the only living thing that's consistently thrived (except for the children), despite us. Pushed back in the corner of our library/living room—amid shades of green from an old shutter propped up in the window (an idea not quite resolved), green-and-white checked fabric tacked onto frames (easier than curtains), and our treasured Adirondack chair taken down to at least six layers of paint (all of them visible)—it imparts a lush quiet to a more-than-frenetic environment. Enjoying the moment: my "Rasta" rag doll, the creation of the artist Susan McCaslin, in meditation under the tree. Above her, peeping out of the branches, another strange lady—a painted cloth portrait from an earlier age—more straitlaced but funny in a headdress resembling two feathered horns. The base of the ficus is swathed in soft green fabric, and lined up on the window ledge is a collection of blue enamel bowls. The odd-shaped object on the arm of the chair is a hang-up wooden soap dish often mistaken for an ashtray—please, no forest fires allowed!

Remember this challenging childhood game? Hidden in a picture were a bunch of "lost" bunnies or some other obscured objects. Now try this one. There are nine secret gardens in Nell and Hunter's living room, left. Find them. (We won't make you turn the page upside down for answers.) Starting at the back of the room, on the mantel are four—under a portrait of an English gentleman, there's a pair of baskets brimming with herbs; and to the left, an herbal wreath spiked with a white daisylike "everlasting" called xeranthemum; and below, a tiny version of it—the centerpiece of this fine wooden mantel, which was laboriously scraped almost-clean of its former green paint by Nell. In front of the fireplace, on a delicate French maple stand between two French caned armchairs is the fifth—knotted bunches of lavender in an earthy ironstone mold. (These, and all herbal creations, were brought back from Muskettoe Pointe's herb gardens.) Six and seven are the ficus trees (they shouldn't even count!), and eight's the flowered chenille-covered pillow on the cane-back settee. Underneath, the blue Oriental flowers woven into the rug make nine. We could have stretched our game to eleven—counting the bloom-patterned plates on the Queen Anne dropleaf table and the rococo flowers on the gilded mirrored sconce on the right wall—but we didn't! If you found them anyway, add two extra points.

Right: *In the desert of the Southwest, Georgia O'Keeffe gathered up bits of bleached-out bones. They were her flowers. Homage to her in our living room: a bleached-out skull bedecked with dried flowers, a bridal bouquet from a close friend's wedding.*

FALL

SHELF LIFE

I n our homes there are no secrets. Everything's out of the closet, exposed on shelves. Cups and plates are seen through glass-paned cupboards. Forks, knives, spoons, and all utensils are stored standing up in jugs or mugs. Some may recline in wooden boxes but none (almost) are hidden in drawers. When everything's out in the open, there's no confusion about where things go. But it's more than practicality that guides us—certainly not the need to show off. There's just something warm and reassuring about being surrounded by everyday objects—like a colander hung on a nail.

Left: In our weekend kitchen, this old-fashioned pie safe converts into a modern-day larder crammed with up-to-date foodstuffs—from tea bags to cereals, tin bowls to trays. Security is provided by a see-through screen door and a squadron of folk art. Perched on top: a red-headed bald eagle from down Mexico way, an Ilse Getz cardinal poster tacked to the wall, a ten-gallon hat, and an ever-ripe arrangement of absurd wooden bananas. Lookouts to the left: a black bull of papier-mâché and a cat-and-pig duo in scroll-relief frames.

Left: *In Nell's French-style home with country touches, the real pièce de résistance (or pièces, really) is discovered in the dining room. "It was put together with help from Mother—who else?" reports Nell. "It's just an old English shelf hung over a French side table. I guess you could say they're confidently mismatched." The plates, with the exception of the platter, are an Oriental-flavored set of undetermined origin. The yellowware mixing bowls punctuate the whole collection but seem more in keeping with the majolica and stoneware pitchers grouped, left, on the marble tabletop. The diminutive tea set, a loan from daughter Christian, sits prettily in front of a strutting wooden cock and yet another Muskettoe Pointe wreath pasteled with touches of pink globe amaranth, tiny rosebuds, and a flowered tile. On either side are perched a pair of framed bird prints. The upside-down water goblets serve no particular purpose. "Except," puts in Nell, "I like the way they look, and they're handy to the dining-room table." Parked beneath, another worthy family tool, a French wooden dough tray lined with long-stemmed yarrow. At the very top, an original watermelon slice by the Virginia folk artist Miles Carpenter. The rush-seat chairs aren't French or old but Haitian imports lightly whitewashed by Nell.*

Above: *A place-mat island of tabletop staples floats on a red-and-white checked vinyl sea. In the center, a no-nonsense wooden box with a watermelon grin has standing room only for forks, knives, and spoons—and napkins in the rear. From left to right: a yellow ducky pitcher dispensing soda straws, a red plastic salt-and-pepper two-seater, a white china sugar shed with a top and a spoon, a 1933 cookbook on baking—a house gift (hint?) from a friend, and a heavy-duty cast-iron pepper grinder from London.*

Left: *Making a rare appearance in a Carter home, a real kitchen cabinet with an open-door policy and a record ear of corn. Lined up on the real "cup board" below, left to right, a family of pitchers, a porcelain tea strainer, a watermelon crop of cups, a restaurant-style stainless-steel creamer, brown earthenware custard cups, and three ironstone dishes—the last, a nest for a wiry bird.*

Prizes above a sink in our city kitchen: left to right, a pair of "reassuring" colanders; store-bought potholders next to a handmade treasure hooked up with a cookie-dough basket of flowers; a cookie puss; a "sageprint"; a collection of antique enamel spoons, ladles, and skimmers; above them, a painted-tin turtle mold; an Indian postcard; a miniature sconce above an old scrub brush; a coiled wire egg strainer; a spongy green dinosaur.

Left: *The first thing we did to our city apartment kitchen thirteen years ago was replace its conventional 1950s metal cabinets with these open-air graduated shelves. They store and display everyday crockery and spongeware.*

Above: *Many early cupboards were built to conform to the architectural lines of a room. This half of one, unearthed in a junk shop in North Carolina, is a bit nonconformist, hung from a wall in Musket-toe Pointe's former herb shop, now drying barn. Missing panes of glass allow a nonreflective view of yet more white dishes. Why white? "Because," says Mother, "we always seem to need so much and white is easy to match. It doesn't have to be ironstone. We mix old and new—whatever we find." Drying upside down from the ceiling beams are, left to right, golden yarrow, orange chrysanthemums, and pale-pink globe amaranth.*

Above: *Like an island of serenity, this graceful pine cupboard, once painted red, harboring hoards of ironstone and silverware, presides over a cooking storm in Muskettoe Pointe's kitchen.*

Right: *A five-foot-by-three-foot pine cupboard, just the right size for a small city kitchen, opens its doors to reveal an upstairs array of plain and patterned ironstone—plates, platters, bowls, and matching tea set. Down in the cellar—a stockpile of supermarket staples.*

Above: *Above two banister chairs is a serviceable plate rack, built by Father one Christmas for Cary, which stores and exhibits three shelves of pewter and pewter look-alikes. The three cups almost centered on the bottom shelf are reproductions of the originals designed by Thomas Jefferson—known as Jefferson cups. After moving to Musket-toe Pointe Farm, we were each presented with our own—initials on one side, "family number" on the other. (Since I'm the oldest, mine is number 1; Cleiland, being the youngest, has cup number 9.) The idea was to cut down on so many cup washings. We were each to use our own cup, wash it, and store it. The children love to find their parent's cup and use it. Some are on view in the cubbyholes, below. By now they look as though they really did come from Jefferson's time.*

Left: *It was Mother's idea that, upon marriage, we should all be given pewter, not silver. "Pewter gets better—duller—with every dishwasher run," she said. "It never breaks and goes with any period of furniture." Case in point, an oldest daughter's sort-of trousseau displayed in a fine pine cupboard presented to her by her new husband.*

Right: *A cubbyhole shelf filled with pewter mugs and Jefferson cups. "Probably an old post-office shelf," suggests Mother, who bought it to separate our socks when we were young.*

FALL

Tools

The tools of this family's trade are the tools of our table. Not that we're cooks by profession, or live by bread alone, it's just that breakfast, lunch, and dinner have become our most important family get-togethers. Except for special occasions, we've given up on setting tables—we just line up and help ourselves. At Muskettoe Pointe, that's half the fun.

Left: *An afternoon tea party at Muskettoe Pointe Farm, thrown by Puppy Dog (center) for his best friend, Bear, and Bear's fiancée, Matilda (both left of Dog). Among the invited, continuing around, were Cabbage Patch Kid (who spilled his tea) and two fine ladies propped up on pillows. The two kinds of cookies—fruitcake and sugar—were contributed by Liza, and the tea, served from an unconventional set (scraped together by the children), was an herbal brew grown in the garden. The old-fashioned ice-cream-parlor spoons seen on the preceding pages and set on the table were a pre-wedding gift to the loving couple. Bear sits on a child's homemade chair and the ladies on a Chippendale miniature. The weathered twig table was brought in from the yard.*

Preceding illustration: *A family obsession—spoons! The five to the left—the pewteriest pewter—were a Christmas present to Mother from me. The crooked-old, warped-old pewter soup spoon in the center is bent into an almost sculptural form. The nest of baby spoons, right, the stars of the tea-party table, were the turn-of-the-century tin versions of the throwaway plastic ice-cream spoons of today.*

Wooden spoons, a "Mother discovery"—perfect for soup, for stirring, for scrambling eggs in a Teflon pan.

Past their prime, these nine ivory-handled, silver-banded knives will never set a table, but for decoration they're just fine.

Above: *In the seventeenth century, when this saltbox was built, salt wasn't something you threw over your shoulder, which accounts for the design precautions the artisans took. The splayed legs make it practically impossible to turn over. Its final test is in the kitchen of Muskettoe Pointe Farm, where it has become an extra stool, a footrest, and a table. The salt crock, on top, hangs from a nail in the kitchen wall. It stores everything but salt.*

Right: *Dough trays, made from scooped-out tree trunks, were originally used for kneading bread dough. The larger ones, standing up to four feet, we line with giant plastic lawn bags, fill with ice, and use to chill bottles of wine and canned beverages at large parties. (See our Fourth of July picnic, page 228.) They can also serve huge amounts of bread. Once, at a wedding, we even filled one with a raw vegetable salad. The smaller trays function better indoors. They hold mounting stacks of mail, dried herbs (see Nell's yarrow, page 62), and, if necessary, a bedless baby overnight.*

Above: "Tools for the food," as Mother puts it—dough trays and cutting boards (all different sizes) lined up on a fifteen-foot bench against the sunset side of the Muskettoe Pointe house. "We cut most of them ourselves from old pine for a friend's out-of-town wedding picnic. I didn't want to carry a bunch of breakables, so these served well as plates, platters, tailgate sideboards, and instant picnic tables." At home (see page 200-201), they're used daily to cover up and transform a kitchen countertop-cum-sink into temporary quarters for serve-yourself meals.

Right: Pots once used for storing cheese or Pooh Bear's honey now do nothing but show off on a narrow shelf above a regiment of working-class red cookware, below right.

FALL

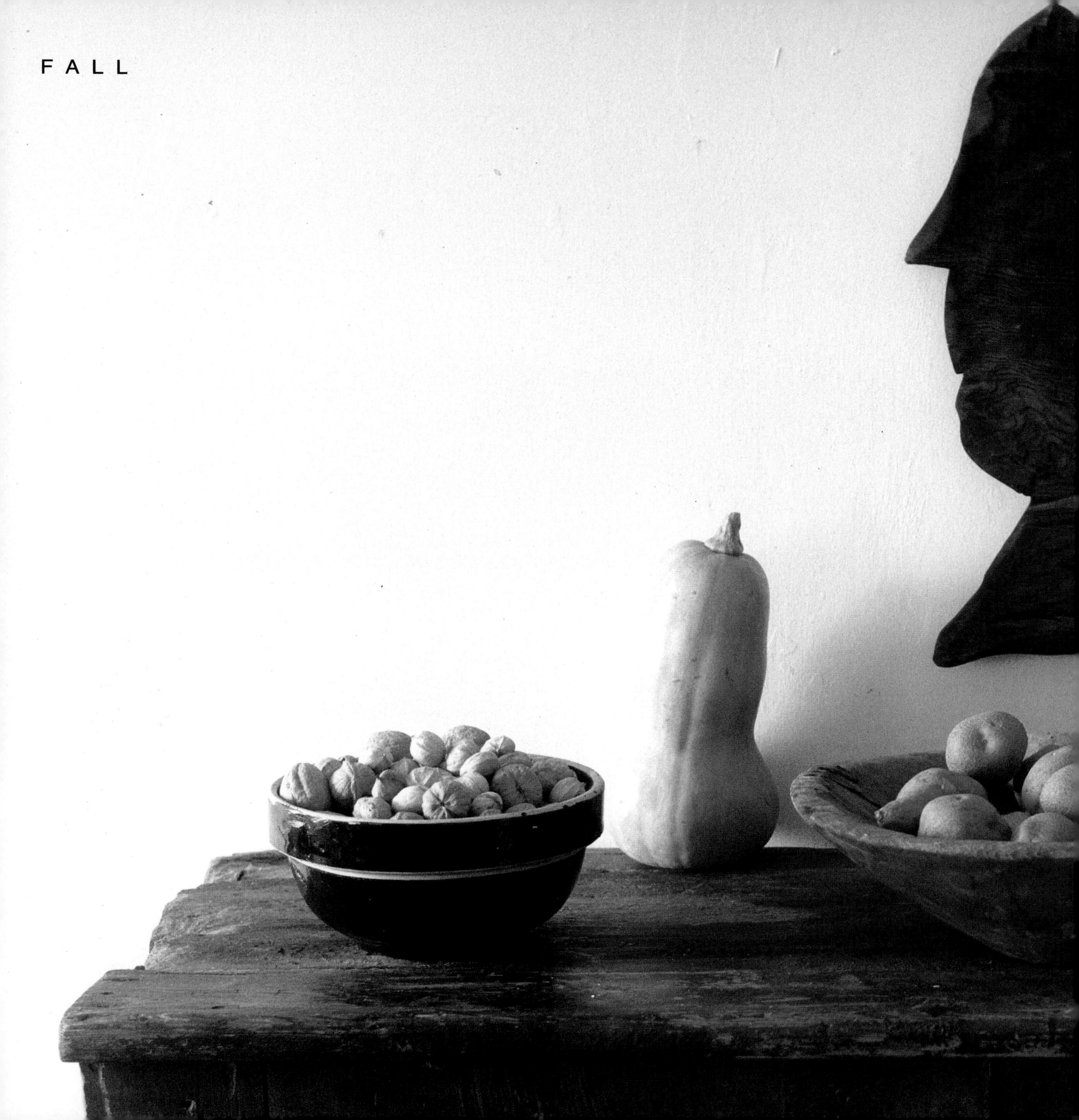

THANKSGIVING

A year and seventeen days before the Pilgrims landed, the first official Thanksgiving was celebrated in Virginia on the shores of the James River,* just fifty miles southwest of Muskettoe Pointe Farm. The year was 1619. Today, instead of gathering at home, we scatter all over the country to give thanks with spouses' families and friends, inventing traditions of our own.

*Though most of us take for granted that it was the Pilgrims who first celebrated Thanksgiving in New England, others, particularly Clifford Dowdey in *The Great Plantation,* state that it was a group of colonists, sent by a British company to Virginia with the hope of starting America's first industry there, who, on December 4, 1619, gave thanks first. Over three and a half centuries later, the plantation they founded, known today as Berkeley Plantation in Charles City, Virginia, is the yearly site of a commemorative Thanksgiving festival. (For more information and to order a copy of the book, write The Virginia Thanksgiving Festival, Inc., P.O. Box 5132, Richmond, Virginia, 23220.)

Preceding illustration: *Thanksgiving offerings under a hand-carved Indian silhouette: left to right, walnuts, an upright butternut squash, a wooden bowl of yams and potatoes, another squash, and globes of onion.*

78

Far left: *One Carter table—ours, in the country—ready to begin Thanksgiving tryouts. Platters, bowls, molds, a wooden turkey, a cardinal and a blackbird, a pitcher, a cutting board, a dough tray, and condiment movers and shakers abound on this sagging stage. The silver is polished. The knives are sharp. All await starring roles in the greatest (we hope) meal on earth!*

Left: *Cornstalk colors reflected in earthy crockery, bowls, and saucers. The platter, front left, originally white, got spattered in an inadvertent baking. The folk-art turkey and two birds are by Miles Carpenter. The hand-painted pitcher, far right, a substitute gravy boat, was carried by hand all the way from Sussex, England.*

Bottom left: *Meanwhile, back in Virginia, at Muskettoe Pointe Farm, a bowl of yams awaits its turn to stir up some fun in a Thanksgiving sweet potato pudding. (Recipe, page 86.)*

Bottom right: *One little, two little, three little Indians (the third, not quite seen, is on the preceding pages)—hand-carved, wayward wooden pieces found in a yard of cast-cement artifacts.*

79

It's the day of the kitchen. The smells and the sounds are tantalizing. The children keep coming—"I'm hungry. When's dinner?"

"Soon, soon. Eat walnuts and raisins. Who's winning?"

Too many cooks, but that's half the fun. Friends stop by and join in the melee. And still the children and now some grownups plead: "When's dinner? We're starving!" It's a crisp day. Beautiful. Feelings of thanks are in the air.

There are divisions of labor: some set the table, some baste and stir, some stay glued to football and report the scores. There's a fire in the fireplace. Everything's cozy. Then, "Dinner is served," greeted by hurrahs and hollers and a friendly stampede. The children jostle for position and plates. Silence for a moment—for thank-yous and memories.

Preceding illustration: *A bountiful table of all-American food served in the shadow of a folk-art metal flag, a potful of eucalyptus, and a pair of exotic birds propped in front of windows to screen out the cold.*

Left: *On Thanksgiving weekend, we head for the country and farm-fresh mountain greenery: a lineup of bagged brussels sprouts and green beans, acorn squash in a green crockery bowl, and a spray of spring onions. The unusual round oil painting of man's best friend with a bird held gently in his mouth does* not *portray the one we'll roast for dinner!*

Above: *A Monet-like miniature of floating brussels-sprout leaves. Casting off these outer layers sets up the sprouts for a better-tasting steam. (Recipe, page 84.)*

THANKSGIVING GRAVY

When I have to go Thanksgiving on my own, without Liza or Mom or Nell or Cary—all good gravy makers—I've been known (shhh) to pick up some powdered onion-soup mix and follow the gravy directions on the envelope. Now that I have (at last) a family recipe, I guess I won't have to (whew!).

Turkey giblets and neck
3 cups water
¹/₂ cup all-purpose flour
Salt and pepper to taste
Heavy cream (optional)

Place turkey giblets and neck in a medium saucepan with enough water to cover (about 3 cups). Simmer, covered, 1 hour or until tender, then strain, reserving broth. Pour drippings from the turkey roasting pan into a medium-size bowl or 4-cup measure and let stand until fat separates from juice. Skim ¹/₂ cup fat from separated drippings and pour fat back into roasting pan over medium-high heat, adding flour and stirring and scraping to incorporate turkey bits until mixture is golden brown, about 3–4 minutes. Skim remaining fat from drippings and combine the unfatted juice with reserved giblet broth. Add about 4 cups of the juice-broth mixture to flour mixture in pan and cook, stirring constantly, until mixture is thick and smooth. Season with salt and pepper. A little cream can be added to make a richer gravy.

Yields approximately 4-5 cups of gravy.

DADDY-MADE-US-LOVE-'EM BRUSSELS SPROUTS (with Ginger)

Daddy taught us long ago to love all those weird and wicked (yucky, our kids call them) green vegetables like turnip greens, collard greens, okra, and brussels sprouts. Though we prefer the latter served up simply with just a little melted butter, salt, and pepper, the ginger takes the edge off and makes them almost exotic.

2 pounds brussels sprouts
5 tablespoons butter
2 teaspoons minced peeled fresh ginger
1 tablespoon lemon juice
Salt and pepper to taste

Remove outer leaves of brussels sprouts (and make a still life if you wish; see page 83), then cut a small cross in the stem ends. Wash sprouts well, then steam them over well-salted water until tender—about 8–10 minutes. Drain and rinse well under cold water. Shortly before serving, melt butter in a large skillet. Add minced ginger and cook over moderate heat 2 minutes. Add sprouts and toss gently until warmed through. Add lemon juice and toss. Season with salt and pepper.

Serves eight to ten.

JOHN'S APPLE-SAUSAGE STUFFING

John's introduction to the family (on Liza's arm) was a Thanksgiving dinner. He carved the turkey splendidly, won our approval, and next Thanksgiving produced this stuffing.

8 cups bread, two to three days old, crustless and cut into ¹/₂-inch cubes
1 tablespoon poultry seasoning
1 tablespoon dried sage
4 tablespoons chopped fresh parsley
2 cups diced onions
1¹/₂ cups celery, chopped
7¹/₂ tablespoons butter
¹/₂ pound bulk pork sausage
³/₄ cup chopped pecans
2 cups tart apples, unpeeled, cored, and chopped
1 cup chicken broth
Salt and pepper to taste

Bread should be rather dry. If moist, put cubes on a cookie sheet and toast in a preheated 350-degree oven 12–15 minutes, tossing the bread every 5 minutes.

Put bread in a large mixing bowl and sprinkle with poultry seasoning. Toss gently. Sprinkle sage and parsley over bread and toss. Sauté onions and celery in 1¹/₂ tablespoons butter until limp. Add to bread mixture. Cook sausage, breaking it into bits as it cooks, drain, and add to bread. Melt rest of butter in chicken broth over medium heat and pour over bread mixture. Toss. Add pecans and apples and salt and pepper to taste. Cook inside turkey or in a greased, uncovered casserole in a preheated 350-degree oven 1 hour.

Serves ten to twelve.

BERRY SHERRY JELLY

Here's Liza's variation on wine jelly, a big southern tradition. We see it as one more way to get cranberries into Thanksgiving—a sort of tart cranberry dessert that could be served with whipped cream. Looped and piled with glazed green and purple grapes, it adds a bit of cool, shimmering elegance to a basically warm and earthy table.

1 3-ounce package raspberry gelatin
1 cup boiling water
2 envelopes unflavored gelatin
2¹/₂ cups cranberry juice, unsweetened
1 cup dry sherry
4 tablespoons lemon juice
1 egg white
¹/₂ pound green seedless grapes
¹/₂ pound purple grapes
¹/₂ cup sugar

Put raspberry gelatin in a large bowl with boiling water and stir until dissolved. In another bowl, sprinkle unflavored gelatin over ¹/₂ cup cranberry juice to soften. Bring remaining cranberry juice to a boil, adding the cranberry gelatin mixture to it. Stir until dissolved. Then pour into the bowl of raspberry gelatin. Mix in dry sherry and lemon juice. Pour into a 5-cup mold and chill until firm (up to 4 hours or overnight). Before serving, beat egg white until frothy and dip in it clusters of grapes until skins are coated. Dip grapes in sugar until glazed. Pile a bunch in the cavity of the unmolded jelly and festoon the circumference.

Serves ten to twelve.

SWEET POTATO PUDDING

The only reason we ate sweet potatoes at Thanksgiving (the only time we ever had them) was because we enjoyed the marshmallows browned on top. They're omitted from this recipe, but if you're planning on tantalizing the children, be our guest.

6 sweet potatoes, boiled until tender, then peeled
12 tablespoons unsalted butter
Grated rind of two lemons
Salt and pepper to taste
¹/₄ cup brandy
1 pint heavy cream
4 tablespoons unsalted butter

In a food processor, puree warm potatoes and butter. Add lemon rind, salt, pepper, and brandy. Beat heavy cream until soft peaks form, then fold into potato mixture. Pour into a greased casserole, top with additional butter, and bake uncovered in a preheated 375-degree oven 30 minutes or until lightly browned.

Serves ten to twelve.

APPLE-CRANBERRY CRUNCH

Rosalie, a good friend from college days, brought the original to a Thanksgiving we once shared. I, in turn, passed the recipe along to the family. It's a crunchy alternative to cranberry sauce. Almost like dessert.

3 cups McIntosh apples, chopped but unpeeled
2 cups cranberries, washed
³/₄ cup granulated sugar
¹/₃ cup all-purpose flour
¹/₂ cup light brown sugar
³/₄ cup chopped pecans
1¹/₂ cups rolled oats
1 stick butter, melted

Mix apples, cranberries, and granulated sugar and place in bottom of an ungreased shallow casserole or tart pan. Mix remaining ingredients and crumble on top of fruit. Press lightly. Bake, uncovered, in a preheated 350-degree oven 45 minutes.

Serves fifteen to twenty.

TURKEY-LURKEY PUMPKIN PIE

It's not Thanksgiving without it. To make your own turkey-lurkey, be creative with a little piecrust. Liza does it free-form, except for the crinkled edge of a cookie cutter to "corrugate" the leaves and tail feathers. Bake these separately, not on the pie, until brown. Arrange on top as you like after the pie has cooled.

2 cups canned or cooked fresh pumpkin
¹/₃ cup dark brown sugar
¹/₃ cup granulated sugar
¹/₂ teaspoon salt
1 teaspoon ground ginger
1 teaspoon cinnamon
¹/₄ teaspoon grated nutmeg
¹/₄ teaspoon ground cloves
3 eggs, lightly beaten
1¹/₂ cups heavy cream

In a large mixing bowl, thoroughly combine all ingredients. Pour into an unbaked 9-inch pastry shell, or make your own from scratch (see piecrust recipe, page 37). Bake in a preheated 400-degree oven 50–60 minutes, until firm. To check doneness, insert knife in center of pie. If it comes out clean, the pie is done. Let cool before serving.

Serves eight to ten.

Thanksgiving goodies—Sweet Potato Pudding, above left, and Apple-Cranberry Crunch, above right. Another turkey to end our meal decorates Turkey-Lurkey Pumpkin Pie, right.

WINTER

WHITES

As winter closes in and snow begins to fall, it's as if it had fallen inside our houses, leaving whitewashed trails on tables, in sinks, along dresser tops, in beds, on ceilings, and on walls. White's always been our chosen color for everything from plates to soap to paper towels. Mother put her finger on it: "It's just so much simpler. Everything matches." She even keeps a bag of white things handy—old damask tablecloths, Spanish shawls, monogrammed linen hand towels, pieces of tatting, and pretty old fringe. The towels make pillowcases for living-room chairs, an old piece of fringe does up a tester bed, the tablecloths welcome guests as special bedspreads.

We had a red bedroom once, and lots of dark-green wallpaper, and even some wallpaper with faded roses on it in Great-Aunt Nell's third-floor bedroom. (She gave us fat red crayons to brighten it up.) Muskettoe Pointe changed all that. The walls are stroked with whitewash the color of oyster shells. Rich browns, green grays and blues, a Chinese red—colors borrowed from colonial times—outline doorways, windows, chair rails, and trim. In contrast—polished floors, early wooden furniture, crocks of herbs, a few simple paintings, shelves of pewter, and people, of course.

Though white accentuates chocolate handprints, scribbled phone numbers, smoke from fireplaces, crayon-streaked murals . . . we still adore it.

Left: *The children said these were snowflakes, so we put them in the window to keep a lookout for the real thing.*

Above: *A winter Valentine—a heart-shaped wreath pierced with a snowy milkweed pod—sends love from a simple farmhouse door.*

Winter light reflects on a still life of kitchen classics in wood and white: a porcelain sink, a scrub brush, a wooden tray, paper towels, and a salad spinner.

Soapy sculptures exhibited in an ironstone saucer.

Room fresheners: open windows, white walls, white towels.

"Scrambled, fried, or boiled?" A pileup of eggs awaits a reply.

A floury flotilla of untrimmed piecrusts on a dusty white farm table.

A cap by the artist Keith Haring and a milky mustache by Carter.

Breakfast whites: mugs, milk, napkins, sugar, vitamins, and cereal.

After the layers of wallpaper were scraped off and a new coat of white went on, after John Marshall got hung, after the furniture and ironstone got placed—a hidden artwork (a gift from the sun) appeared on Cary's dining-room wall—a shadowy silhouette of an indoor tree. (Now you see it, now you don't.)

Above: *No Mad Hatters allowed at this tea party atop baby Mary Ran-dolph's pine dresser. A waistcoated rabbit, far right, did drop in, as did another, much younger—seated in a cushioned rocking chair, left, across from a tiny teddy that shares with him a sumptuous make-believe tea-party feast. The tablecloth, made by Liza for M.R.'s first birthday, is cotton gauze edged in antique lace, as are the cushions. The tea set and the family-style tea party in full swing above it were both found in England. The baby that's outgrown her cradle, by Susan McCaslin, was a gift from a godmother. The tiny tabby in her lap was made from a pattern copied after an early-nineteenth-century cat cousin. The pair of books on top of the pine box are childhood favorites to be read aloud later.*

Left: *Pegged beneath a halo of faded pink globe amaranth, a collection of wool and linen antique baby clothes discovered by Liza in a trunk in the barn. Though they presumably dressed an ancestor's child very stylishly, due to their age and fragility they won't do a thing for our eighties version except decorate her wall. The little enamel heart hung over the middle peg is scented. The ladder-back below it is one of nine scattered throughout Liza and John's apartment.*

Following illustration: *Romantic confections of pinks, whites, and laces geometrically strewn over Liza and John's bedroom dresser. The only masculine touch, upper left corner, is a hint of John's best-loved childhood natural-bristle hairbrush. The pincushion in the foreground, left, looking more like the top of a wedding cake, was made from antique doilies by the aunt of a good friend's friend and given to Liza. The crocheted monogram on the linen place mat includes one of Liza's three initials. Above it, three laminated bird pins and, above them, the inside of the lid of an antique sewing box festooned with test-pattern doilies and a fourteen-sided thread holder. The scallop-edge butterflied hankies, piled at right, metamorphosed out of a flea-market cocoon.*

WARMERS

Think of poor Mole and Ratty, heroes of *The Wind in the Willows,* on the blizzardy night that they made their lost and frozen way through the scary Wild Wood to Mr. Badger's door. In the kitchen, Badger seats the shivery pair in front of the fire and exchanges their wet clothes and boots for warm robes and slippers:

> In the embracing light and warmth, warm and dry at last, with weary legs propped up in front of them, and a suggestive clink of plates being arranged on the table behind, it seemed to the storm-driven animals, now in safe anchorage, that the cold and trackless Wild Wood just left outside was miles and miles away, and all that they had suffered in it a half-forgotten dream.

In winter, when it's cold outside, we all long for Badger's kitchen. We crave the warmth of open fires and flannel sheets or sometimes just warmth's illusion—warm red plaids and flickering yellow flames from votive candles. To warm us from the inside out—soup or stew ladled up from steamy pots and hunks of fresh warmed bread smothered with melting butter. At night, under covers, it's warm milk or cocoa in mugs and lots and lots and lots of hugs.

Left: Brunswick stew fireside at our house in the country (see recipe, page 105). The maître d' hails from Minnesota—a chain-saw sculpture by Barry Pinske. The stew is served in whatever's available—spatterware bowls, coffee cups, custard cups, and crockery.

Left: *Warmer-uppers galore (friends of Rat and Mole, no doubt)—a walking alligator-fish from South America, third row from top; a Miles Carpenter monkey-dog, below right; a slithery polka-dotty snake encircling a juicy (one bite missing) Miles Carpenter slice, below; and, one row down on the far right, a swooping sea gull by W. C. Owens, a wood-carver from North Carolina—make quite a welcome wagon just inside our apartment door. Instead of building a fire (no fireplace!), we light tons of squatty votive candles nestled in mismatched ironstone butter dishes. The flickers and folk art, plus dabs of red on the shelves' outer borders, melt away the shiveriest shivers. If all else fails, there's always the kitchen—not exactly Badger's, but warm and bright, with a checkerboard floor and a resident Holstein cow from Canada, who has a special little candle fire all his own.*

Above right: *"Hands up, you varmint!" A paper cutout villain with paper glove-liner hands (the kind you find inside brand-new dime-store gloves) reaches for the sky as a granny doll watches quietly, undisturbed, from her tiny bench, warmed by red-and-black checked flannel curtains and winter morning sun.*

A tartan flannel pillowcase and an up-to-the-chin sleeping bag keep a ten-year-old third baseman warmed up all night.

Snuggled against a protective shoulder of lumberjack plaid, a hooded and hatted nine-month-old peeks out.

An authentic carriage blanket and vintage L. L. Bean snowshoe chairs turn a week-end bedroom into a sportsman's holiday.

When the mercury drops, we heap our bowls—be they pewter or pottery—with steamy, hearty Brunswick stew. Mother's grandmother made hers in the summer, when all the vegetable ingredients—corn, lima beans, and tomatoes—were readily available. Thanks to refrigerated trucks and frozen foods, we can choose our season. The standard southern version uses chicken, but Great-Grandmother Christian made hers with beef (see recipe below). With bread and butter, it's a meal in itself.

Left: At Muskettoe Pointe Farm, unperturbed by the departure of her luncheon partner, Emily begins her Brunswick stew alone. Well, not quite, if you count the overpowering presence of George III, seated above her. The table is set with pewter, Mason ironstone, yellow napkins, and a warming candle.

GREAT-GRANDMOTHER CHRISTIAN'S BRUNSWICK STEW

2 quarts and 1½ cups cold water
1 cup all-purpose flour
5 pounds stew beef
2 tablespoons salt
Pinch of crushed red pepper
3 large onions, coarsely chopped
4 30-ounce cans whole tomatoes, crushed
2 bay leaves
4 9-ounce packages frozen lima beans
2 cups diced potatoes
4 9-ounce packages frozen corn
1 stick butter
Juice of one lemon
1 tablespoon sugar
Worcestershire sauce to taste

Cook beef in a large, covered pot with 2 quarts water, salt, and red pepper. Simmer about 2 hours, until very tender. Remove meat, then add onions, tomatoes, and bay leaves to stock and simmer 1 hour. Cut meat in chunks, cook lima beans and potatoes separately, then add with beef and corn to stock. Make thickening: in a bowl, add 1½ cups water to flour and beat well until there are no lumps. Add to hot mixture slowly, stirring well so it does not lump. Add butter, lemon juice, and sugar, and season with Worcestershire sauce to taste. Put flame tamer under pot so stew will not stick or burn. Simmer, covered, 30 minutes. Better made the day before and reheated.

Yields 2 gallons.

In an apartment with no room to spare except on the living-room sofa, we still welcome overnight guests (more often in the winter) and try to make them as cozy as possible by banking their unfolded bed, right, with layers of pillows, turning down carefully laid covers (then lights), and offering, along with an alarm clock, a cup of hot milk on extra-cold nights.

Above: *The living room "before." The table and lamp in front of the sofa will be moved to the side.*

Below: *A deep basket once used to hold freshly baked French bread now stores linens, extra blankets, quilts, and a puffy duvet.*

WINTER

PILLOWS

Pillows are our family antidote for hard-edged furniture. Embroidered, painted, created from every kind of remnant—they're lined up, heaped up, hoarded on sofas, chairs, benches, and headboards.

Preceding illustration: *Soft light, three dolls, and home-stuffed pillows smooth the edges of a plain weathered bench against a wall of early pine paneling and whitewash.*

Top left: *On a bed of roses and tulips, two budding pillows, grown from quilt scraps, dwarfed by a double stack of plumped-up feathers. At either end of the headboard, bottom left, more flowers, cradled in the arms of two Mexican maidens. The pair of framed postcards is by the English artist David Hockney. The cat without paws is of South American ancestry.*

Pet pillows, above: A flamboyant bird of paradise nestled next to a terrier. Home to both, right, an Adirondack wonder of variegated colors shaded by two kinds of leaves (from books and a ficus).

111

Top center: *Painted owls, embroidered peacocks, faux tapestry, mad patchwork, needlepoint flowers, and a beaded heart pincushion punch up an all-white sofa.*

Above: *Padding bottoms and backs—a checked flannel leftover, an Indian blanket spinoff, and stenciled vines.*

Top: *Home-grown pillows, including one with a Happy Anniversary message, "Jim & Pat from Liza," to the left of the circle.*

Above: *A doll's settee plumped up with proportioned quilt pillows. A feline variety, made from a pattern, sits erect and standoffish in the center.*

Top: *A pillow made from a doll baby's quilt sprouts tiny ribbons from a fabric bed of flowers.*

Above: *Nourished by the light from a bedroom window, a pillow of tangled embroidery flowers thrives against the back of a green wicker rocker.*

Top: *"Home is where the heart is" reads the sampler on the wall. The heart-stitched pillow below provides a postscript.*

Above: *Patchwork geometry—three circular pillows from yo-yo quilt patches atop a patchwork square coverlet—displayed on a simple cot pushed next to a window.*

Top: *A big bolster pillow placed along the side of a child's trundle will act as a sanitary buffer for a tiny sleeper's head.*

Above: *Beds without headboards have a double reason for lots of pillows. The baby ones dressed in white eyelet and linen are pure decoration.*

Top center: *You'd half expect a sign to read "Please don't step on the pillows." Don't let the lacy handiwork fool you. A minute ago this pristine bower was a changing table for a seven-month-old.*

Above: *Pillows at their best, cushioning the rest of a napping child.*

WINTER

UNDERFOOT

Though the first mistress of Muskettoe Pointe Farm may have dreamed of imported Oriental rugs, it's doubtful her husband could afford them, so other than crawling children and a dog or two she probably kept her floors bare the way we do. The fact is that when we first moved in we did have Orientals—loads of them. Over the years they've disappeared to homes of children, or Mother got tired of them, or the kids, the dog, or time itself chewed them up. In any case, they're gone (for the present). And it's a good thing, too, on this wet, snowy morning. The dining room, below, has been transformed into a bare-bones stage by two desperate moms (Emily and

Liza) searching for diversions for cabin-feverish children. All's set for a "dining-room ramble," our name for spontaneous musical extravaganzas supported by stereo re-creations of Broadway musicals (today it's Mary Martin as Peter Pan). The furniture is pushed back, costumes put on—odd hats and scarves stored for these occasions in a nearby drawer. Sometimes the music is live from an upright piano, hidden like the stereo in a slatted-off annex, as in a colonial tavern. The floors take a beating (there're no rugs to roll up) but whatever harm done is quickly taken care of with some of Muskettoe Pointe's old floor elixir (see recipe, page 117).

Left: A braided rug "pie" of multicolored slivers found at a flea market a decade ago. Probably from the nineteenth century, with its precise geometry it gives an almost modern look to the parquet floor of a city apartment.

The rugs we love spell nothing but trouble. They tend toward old age; they're fragile and slip a lot. We don't include kilims or Orientals in this category because hooked and braided rugs are what we love best. They fit in so well with country-style furnishings, but leave a lot to be desired in terms of durability. Their perfect accessory is another family favorite—stools, not the high ones but the ankle-height bothersomes. They're sprinkled upstairs and downstairs, in bedrooms and living rooms. Painted, upholstered, exotic, romantic—they're used as miniature side tables, in bathrooms for toilet paper, at the foot of large chairs on twenty-four-hour duty.

Above: *Hung out for a sweeping, this huge rag carpet appears to be on exhibit. Popular during the nineteenth century, these hardy floor coverings were made from narrow strips of linen, cotton, or woolen cloth. Look at it again opposite, top row center.*

MUSKETTOE POINTE FARM FLOOR GOO

Loving the way the floors looked in an old mill, Mother once buffed ours with cornmeal. But too much went into the cracks, so she gave up. Any formula that's ever been recommended for old floors we've tried, but nothing has been as successful as the recipe below.

Three parts paint thinner
Two parts boiled linseed oil (a type of linseed oil; you don't boil it!)
One part satin-finish varnish
Colorless paste wax, Johnson's or Bowling Alley

Mix thinner, oil, and varnish well and spread on the floor with a wide paintbrush. Let it sink in for about 30 minutes, depending on how dry the wood is, and wipe off excess with a clean rag. Let the finish dry thoroughly (this could be up to several days, depending upon the weather, condition of floor, etc.). Spread on paste wax with a cloth and buff according to directions on the can. Note: M.P.F. Floor Goo is meant for unfinished floors that need a restorative tonic. The results should be a healthier wood with some sheen helped along by the paste wax. To make sure it's for your floors, test it on one board ahead of time.

Top: *A bedside stool rests on a braided rug.*

Above: *The slot makes this stool portable.*

Top: *A child among needle-point florals.*

Above: *Two for the feet, in funny fabrics.*

Top: *Wiggly rug colors match those above.*

Above: *A patterned footstool mimics a kilim.*

PORTRAITS

A Polaroid of the author, snapped by Brigitte Lacombe, became an earthy Valentine for her husband in a heart-shaped birchbark frame.

Preceding illustration: A photographic chorus line of children and grandchildren on the mantel in Mother and Father's bedroom, except for the baseball-gloved youth sitting on a fence—no kin at all.

W e never had a family album except the ones that our aunt, Sister, filled. She patiently snapped away for years—ten red-and-green leather-bound albums—and then gave up. The other day I picked up a crumpled black-and-white photograph dated July 1955. Seated in a rowboat with her back to the camera was a dark-haired young woman. Next to her, a child, a boy or a girl—it was hard to tell—with a life jacket on and a fishing cap cocked to one side. The two were seated facing two others, in the same life jackets and floppy straw hats. The boat sat in calm, almost flat water with a line of trees and houses on the horizon. There is more to this picture than meets the eye, however. I am the child with her back to the camera, my hair so short I had no

gender. The woman is Mother; the other girls, my sisters Nell and Cary. The picture tells me I am ten and Mother is much younger than I am now. The boat was red; the floppy hats were orange and yellow; the water was no higher than our knees. All of this I knew somehow, but the little piece of paper restored it in a flash.

Snapshots like these jolt our memories. They're our visual fingerprints, pressed onto pages, stored in cardboard boxes, framed with ornate borders, stuck between plastic windows, smooshed in our wallets, even made into books. They glue past to present; sister to brother; wife to husband; son to mother.

Taking pictures can seem a thankless task. Thank you, Sister.

Above left: *A girlhood memento of Howard's mother, Jean, on the beach with her dog, Dodo. The plastic box frame not only preserves the original hand-tinted black-and-white print but gives it a modern touch.* Above center: *Black-and-white photographs have a certain romance to them, especially when they're of your parents as new-lyweds. A cousin found the original among his mother's collection* and had it copied for us children. The frame was painted red on a whim. Above right: *An unknown graduate immortalized in an in-genious frame made of folded and interlocked soft cigarette packs (mostly Pall Malls). A "found" art object dating back to the twenties or thirties, it was probably done as a camp project. A more recent project—the lamp—was made from an old green wine bottle.*

Left: *The way I wish I looked as a child—a cardboard illustration framed on the wall in our country bedroom next to my favorite chair, faded to its present glory by the weather. I found it at an outdoor furniture dump for five dollars.*

Above: *Three styles of portraiture—watercolor reproductions of family life, far left and right, by the Swedish artist Carl Larsson; between them, an unframed oil of Victorian girlhood; and below, a contemporary lineup framed in tiny plastic boxes. The furniture's just as disparate—a primitive green jelly cupboard played off against the formality of a pair of Queen Anne chairs.*

Above: *Nell and Hunter's family reunion of photographs, held in their living room on top of an American stenciled pine dresser, is dramatized by the stirring death of Lord Nelson in the background. Each frame has been particularly chosen for its subject. The World War I soldier, far left (no relation), in an oval tin Photo Medallion that probably sat on his sweetheart's dresser; the two inverted horseshoe shapes framing a just-born Christian, back row, and her mother, Nell, to the right, were touched up with hand-painted details. The blue enamel circle around an older Christian, front row, is edged with lacy filigree. Set apart, far right, is the last picture of Mother's mother, who died not long after it was taken, at age thirty-two.*

Left: *Above the signa-*
ture lamp of a
young history buff,
more historical per-
sonages (all repro-
ductions)—George
Washington and,
above him, Lord Nel-
son. To their left,
framed in red, a he-
roic profile of
Thomas Jefferson.

Opposite page: *Sharing a corner with a papery, berry-stained, bamboo-poled umbrella (used in the summer for garden parties), a heroic George III sits in partial view.* The full view, left, is not the fullest view, however. Supposedly, the original was a full-length portrait, but the bottom somehow became damaged and it was cut and ingeniously reframed by a diligent dealer, which accounts for the rather odd cropping. The tables of the room are an American tavern table of walnut, beneath George, and, in front of the fire, an English oak gateleg with a fresh crock of tarragon. The little nun standing by is Spanish—Saint Teresa of Ávila. The little doorway is only five-and-a-half feet high. The children of the house have always claimed it as their private portal, though more than likely the height was just right for the original residents.*

*Though there has been speculation that this George III could actually be Cornwallis, we choose to believe the former, feeling that, especially in Virginia, people might wonder why we would hang a portrait of Cornwallis, who led the English against us on our own soil, not so many miles from Muskettoe Pointe's front door right on our living-room wall . . .

Right: *We know very little about this sweet young lady, except she's English and we call her Sarah. Her enigmatic smile has earned her the title "the Mona Lisa of Muskettoe Pointe," where she hangs in the living room unfettered by a frame. She keeps an eye on the uncalculated clutter of treasures placed from time to time on top of a tall chest, unreachable by children under a certain height and age. From the left, a very ancient jade-green pot from China—a rather grandiose vase for cinnamon sticks; books—very old, very special, some of them deteriorating already; the small prone object, almost camouflaged in front, is an old gunpowder horn; the hand-blown glass wine bottle from the ruins of Corotoman, the nearby early-seventeenth-century home of Robert "King" Carter, was excavated by our good friend James Wharton and given as a house-warming present; the American Indian bow, in the far left corner, was found in the walls of another Lancaster County home and has a clay grip.*

Below: *If you ask Mom who the bearded gentleman over the dining-room fireplace is, she'll say he's her great-great-grand-father Christian. Ask Dad and the surname changes to Carter. Both agree the maker of the ironstone platters flanking him was Mason. The brass utensils, below—ladles, skimmers, strainers, warmers—are mostly decorative, like the alternating bunches of dried flowers.*

Left: *A little worse for wear, this ornately carved veneer frame surrounds a profile of Beatrice d'Este, originally painted by Leonardo da Vinci. She stares out the library window, inhaling the pungent scent ever wafting from curtains of lavender. On top of the slant-top desk below her, a pair of bronze thoroughbreds supports a single volume, an elongated wooden Madonna prays, and a diminutive mirror reflects daylight brightly bounced from whitewashed plaster walls.*

Below: *The large portrait and the mid-size one to the right Mother calls her Brideshead duo, recalling the dapper heroes of Waugh's* Brideshead Revisited. *The third, bottom right, framed in gilt, is of a man of the cloth from an earlier century.*

TREASURES

The things we cherish—a wooden Indian, a papier-mâché sheep, a collection of Presidents from cereal boxes, a child's version of Alexander Calder, a red toy truck, a French chandelier—have nothing in common except they were handmade or handpicked by another especially for us and given on birthdays, anniversaries, under the tree at Christmas, or for no particular reason except to celebrate the moment.

Far left: *The permanently lopsided posture of this elegantly padded lady produces a quizzical look that says, "I've got a secret." It lies beneath her tattered hemline—a teapot! She is, you see, an American tea caddy—a gift at Christmas from Liza to me.*

Left: *Although it appears to be leaning like the Tower of Pisa, this grandfather clock is actually French, not Italian. A wedding present plucked from the front hall of Muskettoe Pointe by the oldest daughter, its neck and dial were replaced later with more modern versions.*

Left: *A muscular young Indian brave with a feather in his head and a cleft in his chin, carved by a man named Maurice from Duck, North Carolina, stands straight as an arrow in a Manhattan living room. A head-to-toe view can be seen on the opposite page.*

Above: *The Tarahumara Indians, a musically inclined tribe from north-central Mexico, built this violin to play at their various religious celebrations. The mascot of the music is the tiny carved cat whose head is featured at the top of the neck.*

Top: *A pincushion heart from Victorian times becomes pincushion art with a glass bead design—a Valentine to Liza.*

Middle: *The most romantic thing we own—a French candled chandelier vined with perfect replicas of tiny pastel leaves and flowers. To Muskettoe Pointe Farm with love from the mistress of another old Virginia home.*

Bottom: *A doll-size log cabin built and landscaped by the West Virginia artist Russell Gillespie.*

Top: *A gold-leaf eagle ready to soar from his perch atop a circular Federal looking glass (a bit tattered) in the front hall of Muskettoe Pointe Farm.*

Middle: *A stage for flamingos carved out of a clam shell, with a tropical backdrop and clustered shell footlights (a birthday present from Jimmie to me).*

Bottom: *A twig basket with everlasting wooden fruit and a dough bouquet (brought back by a traveling friend from England) is baked hard, like a cookie.*

Top: *One of the early wreaths of Muskettoe Pointe and a poet— Percy Shelley.*

Middle: *Candles and keys— bunched on a mantelpiece beam salvaged from an old rectory in Lancaster County, Virginia.*

Bottom: *In the library at Muskettoe Pointe, a watercolor map of the world (circa unknown) glued to a fantastic wooden globe. "We know very little about it," says Mom with a sigh, "only that it's very old, very heavy, and the grandchildren love to pick at it."*

Top: *Fruit of the vine embossed on a Parisian treasure signed on the bottom by Monsieur K. G. Clément but given as a gift by* une amie *Virginian.*

Middle: *Muskettoe Pointe Farm twenty-five years ago, captured in local clay by the Virginia artist Katharine Jones.*

Bottom: *A curly newspapered sheep in papier-mâché—a gift for Mother made by Liza during her college days.*

Top: *A hand-carved Indian chief stands beside a homey wooden cutout made by Father for the guest-house mantel.*

Middle: *A deep, green, flowered basket hand-painted a long time ago by a dear friend, Miss Carrie Pickett Moore.*

Bottom: *Alexander Calder, photocopied (not forgotten) by a young patron of the arts, who redesigned his clothes with Magic Markers, added a hat, and gave the picture to his mother.*

Top: *Ga-Ga's cookie-heart necklace, made by a grandchild and polyurethaned so she can wear it each Christmas.*

Middle: *The best thing about this hand-carved, 3-D picture of a model Tyrolean kitchen is that everything's forever in its place.*

Bottom: *A homemade circus after Calder's. Made with wire, wood, paint, and lots of five-year-old enthusiasm, it could be a future gift to the Whitney Museum of American Art in New York.*

Top: *An ancient wooden rocking horse named for Robert E. Lee's horse, Traveler, given by a grandmother (not ours) whose grandchildren were all grown.*

Middle: *Cereal-box gifts from the sixties—a plastic collection of United States Presidents from Washington to Kennedy.*

Bottom: *Half a watermelon and chips of ash wood by the Virginia artist/dentist Ross Brumback. His first hand at anything other than ducks . . . and teeth.*

Top: *Books by anybody—there's no better treasure. Parked on top of them, Howard's red toy truck from me—a stand-in for the real one in the country.*

Middle: *A meditative cat carved from wood, on top of a shelf silhouetted against an unfinished sampler, found at a flea market in Connecticut.*

Bottom: *Plaster nest eggs collected in an old wooden measure. Originally snuck under hens to make them lay more, they now fool unsuspecting grandchildren.*

WINTER

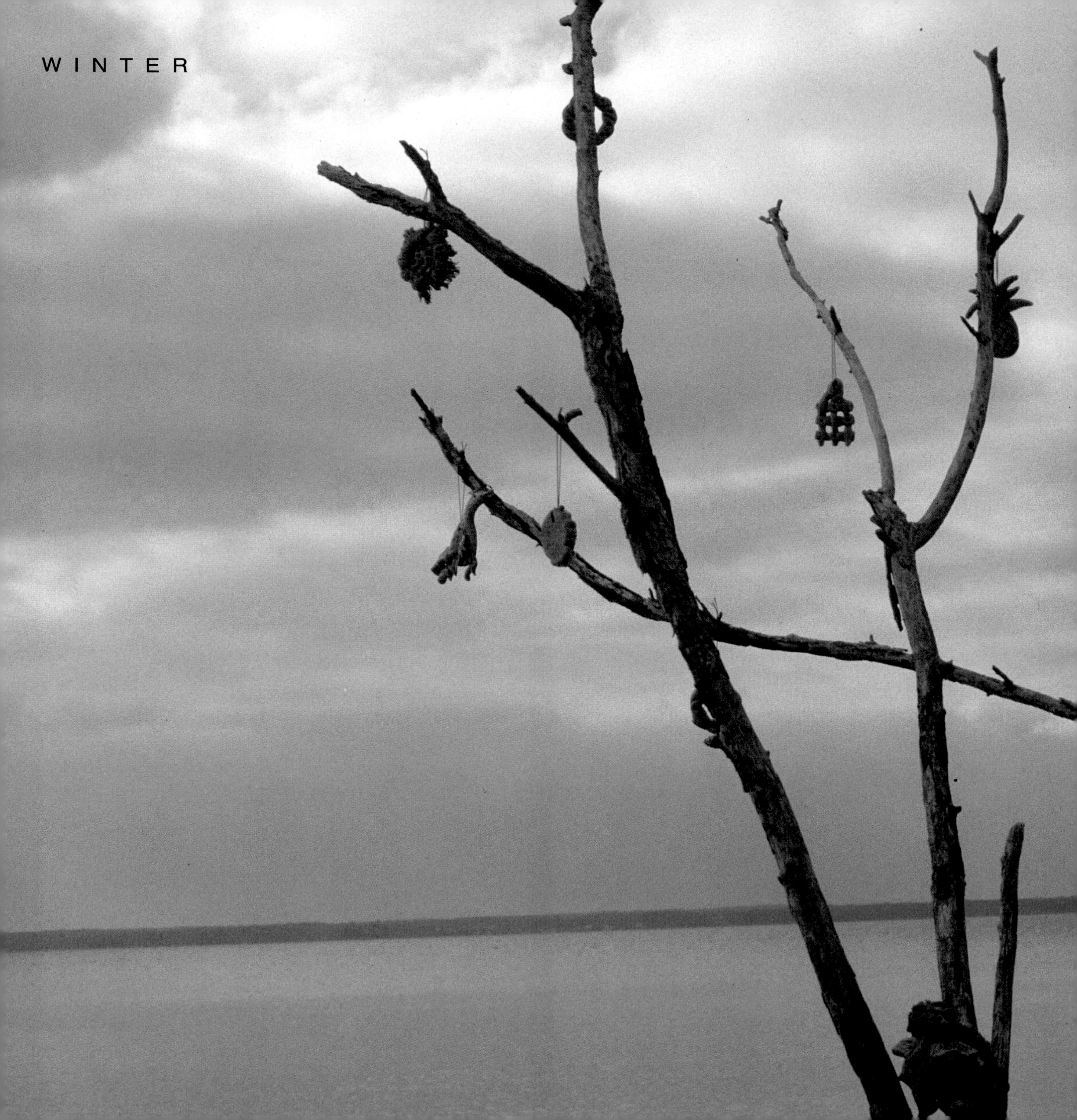

CHRISTMAS

Christmas starts with cookies—to hang, not to eat. Out come the flour, the salt, and the water, the peppercorns, the garlic presses, the rolling pins, the cookie cutters. The flour spreads everywhere. The peppercorns roll. The dough sticks to everything, especially the bowls. Messy hands press and roll and squish and shape until pineapples, a pudgy bear, fantastic creatures, wreaths, and angels bearing an uncanny resemblance to Raggedy Ann appear. On Christmas Eve they will join a cookie cast of hundreds created over the years in Muskettoe Pointe's kitchen to decorate our Christmas trees throughout the house and our driftwood tree on the beach (see previous illustration), created for the gulls, crabs, oysters, and fish that live along the shores of our Rappahannock River. Each Christmas there's another child ready to be told the story of each cookie tree inhabit-ant—how it came to be, who created it, how many Christmases it's survived. This year's newcomer is a cousin of Paddington Bear, dangling at left, made by Cleiland. Ga-Ga, as ever, will wear her Christmas-cookie necklace (see Treasures, page 131), and toot out a tune early Christmas morning through a wrapping-paper-tube horn. The night before, we'll hang our stockings over the fireplace, bake cookies for Santa—the edible kind—and mix up eggnog for our annual grown-ups' all-nighter. Before breakfast, the children's clamor to open the presents will start (once again) in the kitchen. Much later—after the sea of wrapping paper has subsided—friends will drop in to join our ever-widening circle of family and clasp hands with us as we ring the tree 'round and 'round with dancing to our out-of-tune piano, overridden, as always, by high-spirited song and joyous laughter.

Top: *In the kitchen at Muskettoe Pointe, John Christian, left, squishes dough (see recipe, page 137) into a bear-shaped mold (see results, middle) as David adds finishing touches with peppercorns.* Far right: *Cookie camaraderie displayed on a weathered kitchen table.*

Though we all have Christmas trees of our own, in a way they're all practice for the big one at home. In the herb garden, above, a home-grown Christmas tree (a cedar) gets a final saw. The finished product, right, seen early Christmas morn, is wrapped with little white lights (never colored) and hand-strung popcorn and cranberries, and dotted all over with a cookie ornament collection created over the years. Each member of the family has a reserved Christmas-present corner. The youngest children always have places under the tree—which, by the way, is stuck in a water-filled bucket surrounded by a cinder-block fortress swathed in blue homespun. The lights are plugged into a socket upstairs and the cord is snaked through a hole in the ceiling—a year-round spying place for sent-to-bed children.

Left: *An all-natural Christmas tree lit by sunlight only and decorated with strings of additive-free, freshly strung cranberries and just-baked ornaments, including a cluster of grapes, pineapples, and a swan. The roots are intact, hidden in a deep hickory-twig basket. There's only one artificial touch—an ironical one at that—the red plastic heart!*

CHRISTMAS ORNAMENT DOUGH

Though they look good enough to eat, one bite will tell you these cookies are to delight the eye, not the palate.

4 cups all-purpose flour
1 cup salt
¼ cup cinnamon
3 tablespoons nutmeg
2 tablespoons ground cloves
About 1½ cups lukewarm water

Sift dry ingredients together. Add water until dough is the consistency of molding clay. For a better batch, wrap dough in plastic and refrigerate overnight. But if you can't wait, go right ahead! After cookie ornaments are shaped, bake in a preheated 300-degree oven 1 hour. (Dough can be glazed with egg white before baking for a richer color. Though not necessary, a guaranteed way of preserving the ornaments is to brush them with polyurethane after cooling.)

Yields approximately 30 small ornaments.

Above: *A spunky little pine tree dressed to the nines stands on an old English coffer in the middle of Liza and John's ornithological living room. The tree, American grown, boasts an amazing plethora of ornaments, attributable mainly to an eggnog tradition started by John and continued with Liza after their marriage. In exchange for being able to quench that once-a-year thirst for the white creamy stuff and have their fill of Liza's festive cooking and cookies, guests were invited to nurture a collective tree by bringing an ornament each. When the tree reached the saturation point a few years back, the request was suspended, but some (set in their ways at age thirty?) still can't show up empty-handed.*

Left: *The primitive landscape painting locates this tree in our little house in the mountains of upstate New York. There was short-lived debate over whether we should decorate it at all. (My argument was that we'd never had such a perfectly formed tree—decorations might spoil it. I lost.) After hanging lights and our own batch of cookie ornaments, we festooned it with miniature toys, like Carter's acid-green rubber dinosaur (can you find it?). Many were gifts from friends, like the parrot on top, brought back from Trinidad by Una Michaud, a special member of the family for over ten years. (I took the liberty of painting its feathers!) Admiring the tree are a red wooden squirrel from Guatemala, left, with ears like a rabbit's, and, right, an antique lady with a burdensome bonnet from Jamaica.*

Above: *What could make more sense than a tree in the kitchen? Nell and Hunter know—a tree in the kitchen that is well seasoned with red-hot pepper lights. The wreath to the left of the gracefully arched window (Nell's triumphant addition) is wound with a string of cranberries (an idea you'll see repeated on pages to come). The ironstone bowl of crabapples on the table is a festive touch as·long as they last. The red Christmas-tree place mats are brought out for the season.*

Right: *We called this our "Charlie Brown Christmas tree"—it looked so sick and sorry. I kept telling the boys it would get better. I lied. It was a last-minute idea, since we had a big tree (opposite) in the country and one waiting for us in Virginia. We decorated it with leftover cookies, some lions—a new addition, some dried-up red peppers (Nell's had inspired us), some driftwood twigs from summer, and a crowning starfish. I thought the fish decoy above worked swimmingly, suspended from a remnant of an old wrought-iron fence Howard once brought back as a gift from Los Angeles. (He says he bid on it at the Judy Garland auction and won. Insists it was the fence in front of her house in* The Wizard of Oz. *And, of course, I believed him.) The base of the tree is wrapped with that shawl that camouflaged a chair on page 47. The rabbit, a little early for Easter, hopped in from Thailand. The scattered wooden fruit won't spoil while we're away.*

THE NIGHT BEFORE CHRISTMAS AT MUSKETTOE POINTE FARM

(with apologies to Clement Clarke Moore)

'Twas the night before Christmas at Muskettoe Pointe Farm;
The doors were wide open, the fireplace warm.

The stockings were hung by the chimney with care
In hopes that Saint Nicholas soon would be there.

The children were restless getting into their beds
Soon, visions of skateboards raced through their heads.

And I in my Yankee cap, and the rest of the brood
Were just getting into a fine, festive mood,

When all of a sudden there arose such a clatter—
Could it be reindeer footsteps going BANG! *Pitter-patter?*

As I got up to check and was turning around
Down the chimney came Santa, to a chair in one bound.

A twinkle in his eyes and a nod of his head
Reassured me that soon I could go off to bed.

He spoke not a word, but went straight to his work,
And filled all the stockings; then turned with a jerk.

In came the children, wide awake from their sleep,
Some instinct had told them to come down for a peep.

140

He gave them their stockings, then turned to the right
For a stop in the kitchen and a quick morning bite.

But I heard him exclaim, ere he drove out of sight,

HAPPY CHRISTMAS TO ALL, AND TO ALL A GOOD NIGHT!

Early Christmas morning, the kitchen is the gathering spot. The fire has been made. Breakfast is in progress. The children eat nothing. Some are still in pajamas. They stamp around like impatient ponies, waiting for Santa. The faint sound of a carol is heard and then, HO, HO, HO, as a white-bearded, red-suited man—"It's Santa!"—bounds into the room. The older children exchange knowing looks as Santa (who sounds a lot like Uncle Jimmie) leads them, the youngest first, into the Christmas room. Overflowing stockings are distributed and taken back to the kitchen, where the grown-ups, who never seem to lose their appetite, are finishing up breakfast. Candy and toys are strewn over every available surface. Then, time for the official Christmas lineup. (The first one was just a warm-up.) Ga-Ga first (last Christmas was her ninety-first), with Mom and Dad and Sister next. Then, our children, followed by all of us, along with husbands, wives, and special friends. There are yells of delight and choruses of thank-yous as the unwrapping begins and the bedlam continues.

Left: *Cranberry-strung wreaths hanging over Christmas breakfast at Muskettoe Pointe Farm resemble the five Olympic rings, in the Christmas spirit. Seats on either side of the table—a pine settle cushioned in holiday red, left, and a sun-splattered Windsor armchair, right—will soon be taken.*

Above: *Christmas breakfast is shared by just family, so we have no reservations about plunking a pot of grits or a battle-scarred baking pan right on the table. The Staffordshire figurines add an elegant touch, as does the pile of ivory-handled knives in the foreground. From left to right: a platter of fried apples, a molded rice pudding, a pair of Sally Lunn loaves, a dish of herb butter lurking behind the couples, creamed chipped beef, a pan of baked oysters, and, in the orange pot, old-fashioned grits with lots of butter.*

CREAMED CHIPPED BEEF

At Muskettoe Pointe Farm, Sunday's not Sunday without it. Howard had a fit the first time he saw it on the breakfast table—a vision that took him back to the army. After fifteen years of our kind, however, he's a chipped-beef convert.

1 stick butter
1 cup all-purpose flour
1 quart or more milk
3 4-ounce packages chipped or dried beef, chopped
Pepper to taste

Melt butter in a large skillet. Add flour and brown. Stir in milk and then chopped chipped beef. Let simmer until sauce thickens. If too thick, thin with more milk or half-and-half. Spoon over grits or toast.
Serves eight.

HERB BUTTER

We gave up plain butter as soon as the first crop of herbs came up.

1 teaspoon fresh basil
1 teaspoon fresh thyme
1 teaspoon fresh tarragon
1 teaspoon fresh chives
1 teaspoon fresh rosemary
1 cup butter, softened

Chop herbs and cream them into the butter. If you have to substitute dried herbs, use half the quantity specified and sprinkle a little lemon juice over them to perk them up before mixing. Even one fresh herb can make the difference. Spread on hot bread, a piece of beef, broiled chicken, lima beans, green beans, a baked potato—just about anything.

PANNED OYSTERS

At Christmas someone always seems to give Daddy a gallon or two as a present.

¹/₂ stick butter
1 pint drained oysters
Salt to taste
Good shake of red pepper
Good shake of black pepper
1 teaspoon Worcestershire sauce

Melt butter in a skillet. Throw in oysters and let simmer until the edges curl. Add salt, pepper, and Worcestershire sauce to taste. Great with grits, waffles, pancakes, and cornmeal cakes.

Above left: *Chopped up and ready to go—the herbs from our garden that turn plain butter into an herbal delight.*

Above right: *We love homemade bread and knead it often, but must admit that the Sally Lunn loaves on the table opposite were bought from a favorite bakery in Richmond.*

GRITS

Goes without saying . . .

3 cups boiling water
1 cup quick grits
1 tablespoon salt
1 cup or more milk
2 tablespoons butter

Stir grits and salt into boiling water. Use a whisk to prevent any lumps. Simmer 2–4 minutes, then thin with milk to desired consistency. Add butter, cover, and keep warm until serving time.
Serves four to six.

RICE PUDDING

Sometimes it's nice to have something sweet for breakfast. On Christmas morning, call it Christmas pudding.

³/₄ cup uncooked rice
5 cups milk
1 cup water
4 eggs
2 teaspoons vanilla extract
¹/₂ cup sugar
¹/₂ teaspoon nutmeg
1 teaspoon cinnamon
¹/₂ cup raisins
1¹/₂ teaspoons grated lemon rind

Cook rice in 1¹/₂ cups milk and 1 cup water until tender. In a large bowl, lightly beat eggs. Add the remaining milk, vanilla extract, sugar, nutmeg, and cinnamon and mix well. Blend in rice, raisins, and lemon rind. Pour into a buttered Bundt pan or a large casserole. Dot with butter. Place in a larger roasting pan and pour enough hot water to reach halfway up sides of baking dish. Bake in a preheated 350-degree oven, uncovered, 1 hour and 25 minutes, stirring once after 25 minutes. Near end of baking, insert knife in center of custard. If knife comes out clean, pudding is done. Serve warm, room temperature, or slightly chilled.
Serves eight.

From Christmas Day right through to the New Year, friends and neighbors drop in to join us in toasting the season. Thank goodness for Ga-Ga's endless red tins of home-baked cheese biscuits, neatly layered with sheets of wax paper, salted pecans, Christmas "frogs," and fruitcake cookies. The first batch of eggnog, with all the trimmings, is given a warm-up at Liza and John's pre-Christmas "No-gathon." Recipes follow.

GA-GA'S FROGS

1 cup butter, softened
2 teaspoons vanilla extract
2 cups all-purpose flour, sifted
1/4 teaspoon salt
1 cup pecans
2 1/2 cups confectioner's sugar, sifted

In a large mixing bowl, cream butter with an electric mixer, then add 1/2 cup sugar and vanilla extract. Gradually beat in flour and salt. Chop pecans; stir in. Chill dough until firm (about 1 hour), then roll into "fingers" about 2 inches long. Place on an ungreased cookie sheet and bake in a preheated 325-degree oven 20 minutes.

Remove cookies from cookie sheet and place on wire racks to cool slightly. Gently shake slightly warm cookies, 6 at a time, in a plastic bag half filled with confectioner's sugar. Cool the sugar-coated cookies thoroughly on wire racks. Present in cookie tins with wax paper between layers.

Makes 65 cookies.

CHRISTMAS EGGNOG

1 dozen large eggs, separated
2 cups confectioner's sugar
3 cups bourbon or whiskey
1/2 cup rum (light or dark)
1/2 cup brandy
1 pint heavy cream
Pinch of salt
1 pint light cream
Nutmeg, grated

Beat egg yolks at medium speed of electric mixer. Add sugar, beating until creamy. Slowly mix in bourbon, rum, and brandy. Fold in stiffly beaten egg whites, salt, and cream. Chill thoroughly. The longer it stands, the better it gets!

Serves twelve to fourteen.

SALTED PECANS

¹/₂ stick butter
1 pound pecans
¹/₂ teaspoon salt

Melt butter in a large, flat pan in a preheated 300-degree oven. Dump pecans into butter and stir well. Sprinkle with salt. Bake 35 minutes, stirring every 10 minutes so butter doesn't burn.

HOT SPICY PEANUTS

1¹/₂ tablespoons crushed red pepper
5 drops Tabasco sauce
3 tablespoons olive oil
3 cloves garlic
8 ounces peanuts
8 ounces Spanish peanuts
1 teaspoon salt
1¹/₂ teaspoons chili powder
¹/₂ teaspoon curry powder

Heat red pepper and Tabasco sauce in oil 1 minute. Put garlic through a garlic press and add to oil. Toss peanuts with oil and remaining ingredients and cook in a preheated 300-degree oven 30 minutes, stirring every 10 minutes.

GA-GA'S CHEESE BISCUITS

¹/₂ pound butter, softened
¹/₂ pound sharp cheddar cheese (2 cups grated)
¹/₂ pound all-purpose flour (2 cups sifted)
¹/₂ teaspoon salt
¹/₂ teaspoon paprika
Pinch red pepper
Pecans

In a large mixing bowl, cream butter and add grated cheese. Mix well, then add remaining ingredients. Shape dough into 3 rolls, each 1¹/₂ inches in diameter, and seal in plastic wrap. Refrigerate until firm, about 2 hours or overnight. Slice into ¹/₄-inch wafers. Place on ungreased cookie sheet. Press a pecan onto each. Bake 15 minutes in a preheated 350-degree oven.

Makes 90–100 biscuits.

Above: *In the foreground, left, Ga-Ga's cheese biscuits, and right, salted pecans. Behind them, an ironstone bowl of spicy peanuts.*

Top left: *Candlelit Christmas traditions: from the left, Liza's fruitcake; frothy eggnog; and Ga-Ga's once-a-year frogs, slightly dusted in snowy confectioner's sugar.*

In a seventeenth-century environment of pewter plates, an oak settee, and a Queen Anne table, holiday decorations seem somehow intrusive unless kept simple. A silver epergne with pomegranates and lemons, above; right, candlelight via a trio of candlesticks—two silver, one pewter—with a single candle flickering in an old wrought-iron stand; and boughs and vines of anything green—holly, boxwood, mistletoe, ivy—tucked around frames, on mantels, or hanging from rafters demonstrate clearly how simple we mean.

Our substitute for bowls of breakable ornaments—shiny red pome-
granates mixed with grapefruit or lemons. They're kid-proof, non-
breakable, inexpensive, and last (dried) forever.

149

Right: *The mantel in the living room (at Muskettoe Pointe) was once a doorway to a great house in England. One of the dismembered panels went up top, to become the mantelpiece. During Christmas, ivy swags trail from either side and the wreath in the center is festooned with juicy cranberry strings like the ones in the kitchen. Candles lit in the pair of magnificent Waterford candlesticks, protected by ornamented hurricane shades (close-up, left), give off a cheery glow, as does the fire. The embroidered fire screen to the right, next to the armchair, adjusts up or down to protect the sitter's face from the fire. The theme of pomegranates recurs on the center Queen Anne (drop-leaf) gateleg table, lit by a single taper in a towering brass candlestick.*

Top left: *A humble wreath dressed up in cranberry jewelry hobnobs with highbrow Waterford candlesticks graced with dangling lusters and patterned hurricane shades. The bowl below it—English elegance at its finest—is partnered on either side by a minuscule silver-framed portrait of a girl and a hand-painted milk-glass quill holder.*

Bottom left: *Biding their time in a pewter plate, these hand-dipped Christmas candles brighten a table before they're lit!*

Left: *A bird's-eye view of the wreathed bowl on the bench, above right, reveals through its porthole a cargo of onions. Silver King artemisia is burrowed with cockscomb, yarrow, globe amaranth, and lavender.*

Top left: *Hanging from the dining-room window, a swag of Silver King artemisia, tansy, santolina, white statice, celosia, rue, oregano, sage—everything but the garden sink. Emily's directions: Make individual bunches and wrap them together with twine, two bunches at a time, stem to stem. Through the hallway you can catch a glimpse of the wreath, above right, in the kitchen. Decorated with branches of yew, live oak, and apples, it changes its clothes from season to season. The window to its left is a narrow stage, lined with the same variety of greenery, for a flighty cookie angel. Below it, a primitive wooden bench features bowls of fruit and vegetables. The yellow apples, second bowl from right, are wooden.*

Top right: *An international Christmas present from Cleiland to Mother—a family of red-and-white checked French kitchen tins lined up along the bottom of an English hanging cupboard. The wreath, above, dotted with rosebuds, stands out vividly against the Chinese-red background. The red bouquet, below left, is rosebuds and cockscomb.*

Above: *A man for all seasons, but particularly this one—Great-Great-Great-Grandfather Carter (you've met him before under the name of Christian—see page 126). His annual herbal Christmas coronation was started a decade ago. There are some that swear he never smiled until then. The mantel below him is filled with holly.*

Right: *Leaning against a sponge-painted bucket, the temporary lodging for a tabletop tree, a lavender wreath touched up with cinnamon twigs, rosebuds, lavender, and globe amaranth.*

Last Christmas the children, with a little coaxing from their parents, enacted the Nativity scene in the wisteria arbor. The bigger kids, up front, were adoring Wise Men camouflaged in quilts; younger cousins played unruly shepherds; a stoic Joseph and Mary in blue-and-white flannel cradle a multiracial doll found in the attic. The horse, older than all of them, was one of a pair made by Daddy many Christmases ago out of sawhorses, nail kegs, and a good sense of humor.

SPRING

H ERBS & . . .

The real heart of Muskettoe Pointe Farm lies somewhere in its herb garden. The original plan was for a vegetable garden modeled after George Washington's at Mount Vernon. The herbs came later, totally by accident. Mother had bought a pot of chives at the grocery store, and, when she unpotted it, found a clump of a hundred little bulbs, each supporting a single blade. Carefully separating them, she stretched them around a bed of spinach and onions. Later that spring they blossomed with their first purple flowers and by the next had grown into a thick, blooming border. That was it for Mother. Those chives stole her heart. She fell in love with herbs because, she says, "I felt maybe they loved me back."

Above: *Gardening gear ready for duty.* Right: *Flats of new herbs get a head start in the greenhouse added seven years ago.*

That one pot of chives (see an offspring, right, in the center of the second row) caused an herbal coup d'état in the vegetable garden. The first were mainly meant to flavor our cooking—thyme, oregano, marjoram, parsley, dill, sage, and rosemary. But soon, extensive herbal expeditions—to Adelma Simmons's famous gardens in South Coventry, Connecticut; Old Sturbridge Village; and, closer to home, the herb gardens of the National Cathedral in Washington, D.C.—brought back surprising new varieties. They thrived and so did Mother's passion. It overflowed into deep affection for the Garden Club of the Northern Neck and later inspired this herbal ode, written for her by a dear friend, James Wharton, and sung by Mother (to the tune of "I Left My Heart in San Francisco") to any group of gathered gardeners.

> You stole my heart in your herb
>   garden,
> You were so generous with your
>   thyme;
> You always let me eat my fill
> Of wormwood, eglantine, and dill
> While we were testing soil for lime.
>
> I can't express the joys of tasting
> Each spray, each bud, each bush,
>   each vine—
> Your sage remarks oregano thrill
>   me
> With spicy tales of love divine!

Left: *At the herb-garden gate stands a proud little chair, which, in the face of all kinds of humiliations—termite pockmarks, bird droppings, paint splatterings—has survived, dignity intact.*

The kitchen herb garden grows 120 varieties of herbs. Each bed is separated by meandering paths dusted with crushed oyster shells.

Two varieties of santolina—a craggy, sagebrush color in front and a lush, shiny green behind—bloom with a profusion of yellow buttons.

Golden marguerites bloom along the fence that runs beneath the kitchen window. To the right, espaliered on the fence, is Dad's pear tree bearing fruit.

For seasoning food in the kitchen and filling in wreaths and herbal decorations, pungent purple blooming sage reaps double honors.

It was the purply blooms of a clump of chives that set Mother on her unquenchable herbal quest for more, more, more. To the right of the chives is a bunch of violets.

Lean-stalked purple lavender hangs from our windows, colors wreaths, scents potpourri, is the first thing you smell when you enter through our doors.

Snow-in-summer is a newcomer to the garden. Rue, the bluish-green herb that surrounds it, is an old-timer. Changing herbs helps the soil and keeps us interested.

A good place for a breather—a primitive bench in a sea of lavender, santolina, stalks of white garlic chives, and orange butterfly weed.

In May, daisies bloom in the garden along with masses of santolina. The branches of a large magnolia tree are slowly creeping over the fence, left.

Above: *Though the love affair with herbs and gardens was started by Mother, it was soon a passion shared with Dad. While Mom planted seedlings, he planted posts to protect the fledgling garden from furry intruders.*

Top right: *In April, the first flowers to bloom are daffodils and tulips, fragile specks of yellow and red protected by bushy boxwood borders.*

Bottom right: *The wintry skeletal system of an ancient mulberry is haloed from behind by early-blooming forsythia.*

Top left: *By May, the sky and river have turned a vivid blue, the mulberries are sprouting baby leaves, and the gardens are filling up with daisies, lines of purple and yellow irises, and children hunting ladybugs.*

Bottom left: *In June, the gardens are transformed by a kind of lush unruliness. Everything's blooming, but mainly herbs— golden marguerites, yarrow, foxglove, and sage, to name a few. The last vestige of formality is upheld by the garden's center-piece—a multi-tiered holly.*

Below: *May's early bloomers— top, daffodils and periwinkle, and bottom, a brilliant poppy, one of a few planted as an ex-periment.*

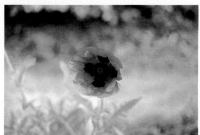

163

The barn, top right, has accommodated everything and everybody, from the original four-legged creatures it was built for to a loft full of overflow sleepers to as many as a hundred varieties of herbs drying from its rafters, right, second picture down. Once word got out that there were herbs to be found at Muskettoe Pointe Farm—in both plant and dried form—hungry gardeners and cooks started showing up. Before long, a family's herbal pastime was turned into a fledgling business, and we sold whatever we didn't use ourselves. Emily, right, third picture down, got busy entwining muscadine grapevine wreaths into herbal wall hangings, left, which are displayed outside the barn along with loaded-down tables of live plant offerings. To these were added those herbal furnishings—potpourri; strings of lavender; baskets, bunches, and swags of everything— that for years had kept our own homes lively with good smells, flavor, and color. We finally got used to the occasional early-morning herb customer, bottom right, who arrives unannounced and is spied through a window happily making his or her way through rows of herbs near the barn beyond the whirlygig at the entrance gate. We've been known (some of us) to take refuge with our first cup of coffee behind the nearest yarrow basket and yell for Emily to come and save us—"There's another herb lover loose in the garden!"

Above: *In front of the barn, where pet horses and a burro used to roam, a field of yarrow now makes a home. After harvesting (by many hands, large and small) it will hang to dry from every available rafter—in the barn, in the log cabin, in at least two dependencies, and above an obliging neighbor's garage. The bench was hand-hewn by Bernard.*

Top: *An "herbwalk" cafe—an umbrella over* tete-a-tete *furniture.*

Above: *Flats of parsley hide their time on the greenhouse floor.*

Top: *Lavender conditioning in a reproduction stoneware pot.*

Above: *A cast-iron pot of geraniums decorates the foot of a post.*

Top: *A barrel of pineapple sage bordered by orange mint.*

Above: *A tabletop garden of five dainty herbs.*

Above: *The playhouse resides over a small working garden of backup herb plants to sell and to transplant to the rest of Muskettoe Pointe's main gardens.*

A potpourri of rose petals, lemon verbena, sage, and cinnamon.

Chive bookmarks pressed between the pages of a scrapbook.

Years of sun have bleached out this globe amaranth.

A standard concocted by Emily of dried sage and rosebuds.

There weren't too many pictures taken at Christian and Christopher's wedding, but her bridal bouquet—made by Emily of tansy, globe amaranth, lavender, sage, lamb's ear, and oregano, caught by Cleiland, and saved by Nell, who hung it over the sideboard (see page 55) in the very room where the couple exchanged their vows—is the most personal reminder of all.

A valance of lavender bunches strung across a bed.

A spongeware bucket of lavender keeps a living room fragrant.

One bunch of lavender is quite enough for this seaworthy pair.

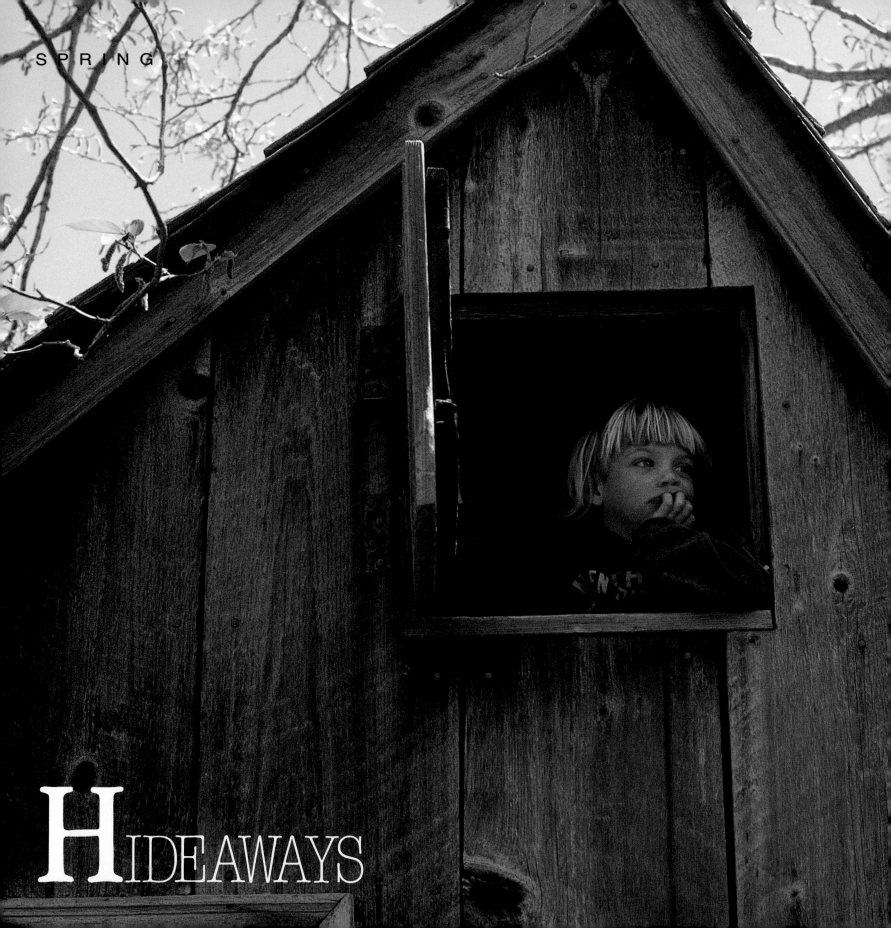

SPRING

HIDEAWAYS

I have a house where I go
    When there's too many people,
I have a house where I go
    Where no one can be;
I have a house where I go,
Where nobody ever says "No";
Where no one says anything—so
    There is no one but me.

The child's house—real or imagined—built in verse by A. A. Milne might have looked, in wood, a little like the playhouse in the children's herb garden at Muskettoe Pointe Farm. One grandchild, left, stares dreamily out its garret window. With so many people—mostly family—always around us, we're constantly scrambling up trees to hide amid their leafy branches or under them for secret trysts in vine-covered arbors. Over not so many acres, many hide-aways have been officially designated. If one is taken, so it is said, the taker's privacy is to be respected. The children have, besides the playhouse, a child-size dollhouse in the attic, at least a half-dozen tree houses, and any place they can squeeze themselves into. For the rest of us, there are the log cabin, the beach house, the barn, and a score of unofficial hideouts we're not allowed to mention. Being a family renegade is pretty serious business.

The arbor, originally built as an outdoor tabernacle for Cary and
Tommy's Muskettoe Pointe wedding, is, twenty years later, almost
completely hidden under thick, twirling vines of leafy wisteria. Its romantic inclinations continue, come springtime, as a trysting place for
afternoon tea served in Great-Grandmother's tea service.

Above: *An apple-blossom sanctuary far from home's wisteria arbor fills the gap for a homesick daughter in upstate New York. Its furnishings—all in shades of green—are almost camouflaged. Left to right: a rudimentary ladderback, a wooden column, an old park bench, and a straw fan-back chair.*

Right: *At the edge of the forest, three ingenious backwoodsmen have strung their army-blanket tent over a clothesline. It's a shady retreat from the heat of the day, unless, of course, it rains.*

173

On a honeysuckled bluff, above, overlooking the river, almost a football field away from the main house, lies Muskettoe Pointe Farm's best-kept secret—the log cabin. Padded by a row of chubby box bushes (see how they've grown in seven years, left) and leaning locust trees, it was built twenty years ago by a family crew led by Benie Robins (a friend of Muskettoe Pointe for many years) and Jimmie. The siding, made of seasoned trapstakes, was filled in with wire mesh and chinked by hand with buckets of concrete mixed in an old tub. According to a worker/witness, the roof rafters were held in place "until Dad okayed the pitch." Between the crowded celebrations—Fourth of July picnics, weddings, and birthdays—it's mostly left alone, even a little neglected. Those who seek a solitary moment, a rest away from the ongoing hubbub, are thankful.

Above: *During warmer weather, the door of the log cabin is always left open. Seen through its summer alternative, a faded blue screen door, is the muslin dust ruffle of the trapstake bed, next page, far right. The roof's wooden shakes have weathered to a silvery gray, as have the logs and the chinking.*

Above: *On the wall opposite the windows stands a mighty fortress of a country cupboard. Both doors open wide to display handmade pottery and brown-papered jelly jars—both Liza's long-ago college projects. The two crocks on the very top and on the very bottom, on either side of the early drawered toolbox, are not.*

Above: *In contrast to the unfinished interior walls, two very finished young ladies,* My Highland Girl, *above, and* Martha, *below, hang near the head of the bed over a very primitive table barely capable of supporting a single pot of rosemary. Though there is some insulation behind the chinking, so far the cabin has no heating.*

Above right: *The cabin bed, blooming with freshly picked locust vines, was constructed of the same trapstakes as the ceiling beams and siding. The mussed-up embroidered coverlet betrays signs of a restless napper or rambunctious children. The candles on the wall, just within reach from the bed's left side, are for nighttime visits.*

Right: *A broader view reveals a well-scrubbed farm table, mismatched chairs, and a triptych view of the river. The basket on the floor and the crock on the table are filled with more locust blooms.*

The beach house, left, the sole surviving structure of River Barn, had been a red storage house (not exactly seventeenth-century), but when painted white and moved to the river it became our perfect wooden beach tower. The name came from a boating friend who would often sail by and spot it sticking out from our bank "like a sore thumb." His simile stuck. The upstairs had always been a summer bedroom, but now, with water lapping beneath its windows, it feels more like a lighthouse keeper's inner sanctum. The downstairs became a screened-in bunk room.

Above: *At the top of the exterior stairway you can peek in through the window and make sure the room is vacant. Through the slatted doorway lies the essence of tranquillity: white walls, weathered floors, two mattresses on boxsprings, a chair, and a table just big enough for books. The only other color is the blue of the Rappahannock.*

Above: *Though we visit the tower room all year 'round, it is in the early spring, when the windows have just been opened, that you feel you could survive up there forever on nothing more than deep breaths of warm salt air.*

Top left: *Taking a rest in the upstairs room of "The Sore Thumb" is nothing but fun for a six-year-old. The wall behind is a row of windows, with the wooden shutters latched to the ceiling.*

Bottom left: *An iron trivet table with rusty feet and just enough room for reading and writing materials stands at the end of the beachhouse pallet made up in softly colored striped sheets.*

Top right: *In summer, the windows facing the river are shaded by bayberry and locust trees. Staring down from there into the water is like looking over the side of a ship—when the wind rocks the house you feel a bit tipsy.*

Bottom right: *A vanished writer has left her mark on both the abandoned bed and the journal. Never fear: she'll turn up. The top of the beach house is the best spot to collect one's thoughts.*

SPRING

BEDSIDE MANNERS

N

ext to our beds: open windows, the smell of flowers, lights for reading and comforting children, piled-up books, unfin-ished diaries, telephone numbers, special mementos, a tree of hats, pictures of family—all these, our guardian angels.

Preceding illustration: *Whoever sleeps in this bed tonight will be soothed by the scent of freshly cut flowers, circulated by the breeze from an open eyebrow window. On the bedside table, actually a small one-drawer desk with a chair drawn up, reside (left to right) a* *pile of well-read magazines, a marmalade pot of purple and white phlox, a child's tin mug with an enamel frieze of dancing bears, and a desperation lamp made from a stoneware bottle topped with an ill-fitting shade.*

Opposite page: *In our city bedroom I've hung my hat on the trapstake bedpost and placed nearby a small image of a Caribbean mother embracing her two sons. It was carved out of a two-toned tropical wood by a Jamaican taxi driver/sculptor named Sam James. He happened to walk into the island shop as I was making the purchase and, upon hearing that it reminded me of my boys back in New York, carved a dedication on the bottom. The blue enamel Scandinavian measuring cup is filled with Virginia yarrow. The pile of books is topped by* The Yearling, *the boys' current bedtime favorite. Under it rests my diary and, on top, a red leather case of French nouns and verbs on miniature index cards.*

Left: *Through the round-topped looking glass at the foot of our bed can be seen a fuller view of my bedside universe. Stationed next to the floor-bound pine cupboard is a dark-green loomed rocker brought back from North Carolina to soothe end-of-day nerves and visiting babies. Up above, orbiting around a two-story shelf of sentimental clutter are, clockwise from the top (between the dusty cloth couple), a toy house with separate entrances for an in-and-out wife and her husband, a pair of owl paintings on glass, a religious tableau painted on tin with a prayer hand-written in Spanish, another painting on glass of a hand and a flower, and a watercolor of the beautiful Indian princess Pocahontas, framed in a gold-leaf oval.*

Above: *At the lacy edge of Liza's side of the bed, a flock of embroidered birds on pillows wing their way toward a bedside English pine desk covered with botanicals of one kind or another. The primitive wooden box on the wall is carved with fanciful figures and the date—1920. The lace-covered pillow below it is part of a pincushion collection.*

Right: *Liza and John's hats for all seasons (reflected in the mirror, opposite page) hang like strange fruit from a fecund Victorian iron hat rack.*

Above: *A bedside trilogy—a glass jug lamp with a lace-covered shade, an ironstone mold with statice, and an intricately carved frame around our World War II hero—Father.*

Left: *Liza owns most of the hats on the hat rack, seen again through the pale-pine mirror edged with an herbal string of dried tansy, yarrow, sage, and lavender. A collection of Victorian flower prints hangs alongside them in a vertical six-framer. More flowers, in porcelain, edge the top of a pair of lean-to mirrors on the pine dresser and a budding majolica pitcher. The pink doily-covered sewing box was seen close up on pages 98-99.*

185

Above: *Up against whitewashed boards in Mom and Dad's bedroom at Muskettoe Pointe stands the original trapstake bed. Above it hangs a wreathed and weathered Indian chief photographed in the early twentieth century by the American photographer Edward S. Curtis. A picture of an unknown Victorian lady is tenuously balanced on the headboard below it.*

Right: *Mother solved her telephone-number problem years ago by throwing out the book (which was always lost and always changing) and writing all the important numbers right on the wall above the phone next to her bed. Some people are a little shocked, especially children brought up not to scribble on the walls, but those of us who share the problem applaud her audacity and practicality.*

On the wall opposite Mother's graffiti-style telephone book stands the desolée *mantel. The name was derived from the tearful situations and people exhibited above it—mainly, the large tinted engraving of a doomed French king taking leave of his sobbing family and the equally tragic pair to the right—Josephine, above, and Napoleon, below her. A little out of place, unless as a memorial tribute, is the miniature wreath propped between them. The mantel itself was saved (unlike the king) from a demolished house in Surrey County, Virginia. The statue of Mary and Child on the dresser, right, was a present. The straw hat and the pearls will, we hope, be found again at Easter. The gold-leaf mirror reflects an unmade bed and a secret hello from a child's sticky handprint.*

Left: *At Cary's bed-side, books hoist up a dainty flower-encrusted lamp which was too low for reading. The walls and bed are splashed with the faint pastels of two sandy seascapes, a layer of patchwork pillows, and a rabbit.*

Above: *When daughter Holly opted for a larger, more modern desk, Cary inherited the quainter version. The letter fence and the cubby-hole at the back were pieced on by Father when the table was originally converted into a desk. Settled into its new quarters at the foot of Cary's four-poster, it's become a three-dimensional family album. Throwing some light on the subjects is a modernized oil lamp romanticized by a cutout shade.*

Above: *During Cary Hunter's temporary residence in the upstairs library, right, Mom Nell cleared a shelf of books (except for a few fit for the baby) and arranged it with more comforting bedside baby stuff (left to right): a candlestick lamp that served as an extra-large night light; a less-than-infant-size tea set—a gift from an aunt recently in Mexico; a framed postcard of a bare-breasted "La Dame de Beauté"—Agnes Sorel, a favorite of Charles VII—passing here as a nursing mother; another framed card, sent by Aunt Liza, of a golden-haired girl and her pet Saint Bernard (in memory of ours); a pottery songbird; a tiny bowl; and a backdrop of Paris.*

Right: *When a baby's hungry, all manners are suspended, so while her bottle's warming up, a note about the bed. It's a Victorian heirloom given to Mom and Dad just in time for the grandchildren. In ten years, it's slept seven—not bad.*

SPRING

V ESSELS

Crocks, pots, jars, jugs, bottles, pitchers, tea pots, coffeepots, creamers, cups, mugs, tumblers, goblets, cans, buckets—almost anything that will hold water we count as vases for the cut things from our gardens, fields, and (sometimes) florists. At Muskettoe Pointe, containers are made of simpler stuff—mostly stoneware and pewter. In some of our homes, we've gone a bit further, filching more ornate ideas from the art of Carl Larsson and the English style known as Bloomsbury.

Left: *The sensual scene of a young girl studying herself in the mirror is a reproduction of a painting by Balthus. The pale-blue pitcher on the mantelpiece before her, in our homes, would hold flowers—like the little rainbow pastel-striped creamer, right, holding the only surviving tulips from a bigger display in another room. Their days are numbered, too (note the fallen petal below), but while they last they bring a welcome insouciance to this functional environment. The succulent plant on the opposite corner thrives in a baroque kind of flowerpot encrusted with flowering vines and flying cupids. The drinking cup is pewter; the shaving brush English. A trio of pastel-colored soap cakes was coordinated with the flowers. The slightly familiar shape up above, displaying a glued-down assortment of shells, is the top half of a yellowed egg carton—a five-year-old piece of nursery-school art.*

Preceding illustration: *In a room reminiscent of a Carl Larsson watercolor (two prints by the Swedish artist hang on the back wall), the main event is the Italian painted urn, bought at a junk sale for under ten dollars. It's filled with purple milkweed, a sweet-smelling wildflower that grows rampant in late spring and early summer near our orchard house. The old scrubbed farm table is covered in the center with a rag-rug remnant. The wooden duck family are waddlers from India. The planked-back bench, one of a pair, was picked up at a street sale in a town along the Hudson River. Through the doorway to the left lies the sun room—an extra bedroom or napping place in the summer. The yellow sea grass armchair is cushioned with a quilt.*

A muddle of lilacs, postcards, favorite people, artists, books, writing
implements, and receptacles artfully arranged by the owner so she
can pick out what she's searching for in an instant. Where are the
paper clips? In the two handmade glazed cups, center; one's white,
the other turquoise. There's a little paperweight duck (by W. C. Owens)
between them. Felt-tip markers? In the big red paper cup taped with a
family Polaroid, in front of the Modigliani mother and child. The
lilac display, far left, in a big tin can that once held Italian tomatoes,
was a happy accident that occurred when nothing else could be
found to put the bouquet in.

A visit to Charleston Farmhouse, the English countryside residence of Vanessa and Clive Bell (Vanessa was Virginia Woolf's sister), Duncan Grant, and various writers and artists who formed what's now known as the Bloomsbury group, inspired the purchase of the pitcher, above, spouting a flowery sculpture of lilacs. The cork-topped glass matador and his lady, left, were bottles for Spanish wine. The tiny matador between them is a doll added later. The matching jars with blue metal lids are bins for stray buttons, pins, and broken earrings. The flamingo thingamajig, right, was counted among the family treasures on page 130.

A blue enamel Dutch coffeepot serves up a helping of early spring tulips. One becomes an eyepatch to a cement girl already wearing her Easter bonnet.

An old galvanized bucket filled to the brim with frothy to-be-dried hydrangeas.

Settled into an old wooden toolbox (missing the top), a family of purple cabbages crane their wiry necks toward the sun.

A mottled blue-and-black tin coffee percolator, brimming with wild lavender and white phlox, makes a regal centerpiece for an outdoor dinner table.

Blooming tentacles of bridal wreath reach out from a stoneware crock. A brown glazed pot, left, awaits a similar treatment.

A primaveral wreath of grape-vines and lilacs nailed onto a whitewashed wide-board door.

A cherub-clustered canister stores, instead of tea, a fresh crop of zinnias on top of a kitchen stove.

Right: *On warmer spring days, the double front doors of Musket-toe Pointe Farm are pushed open to welcome still-fragile sunlight into the front hall. It glints off a fine blue-and-white English punch bowl, a cherished parting gift from a neighbor who had lent it so often that, when she moved, she felt the bowl had to stay. It shares the top of an oak blanket chest with an earthy stoneware preserve jar filled with white wild yarrow and oregano from the garden.*

Below right: *Another view of Mus-kettoe Pointe's dining room, the scene of year-round dancing (see page 115) and eating. The wood-slatted annex to the right of the grandfather clock was cop-ied after the keeping room of a colonial tavern. The cupboard inside, displaying Mason iron-stone plates, hides a stereo below. An old upright piano stands op-posite. The tall, skinny French wing chair, right, is one of a pair sought after when a fire is blaz-ing in the fireplace. Until several years ago, however, the fireplace was unplastered and the ceiling unpainted. The gateleg table is one of several set up in the room when a crowd is dining. The chairs are Windsor and Queen Anne—a mixture from the eigh-teenth century. Boughs of herbs hang from the ceiling, along with a tin chandelier down to one candle nub.*

198

Left: *A rustic twig table set with a majolica pitcher of Queen Anne's lace is the springtime replacement for a potbellied stove hooked up in winter to the flue now hidden behind the picture. Muslin curtains hung from unpainted dowels do a poor job of blocking the sunlight that pours year-round into this country attic bedroom.*

Below left: *This brown glazed stoneware pot, lidded, might have stored herbs, spices, honey, cheese, or even beans. Today, squished with Oasis,* it holds golden marguerites, purple loose-strife, and salvia Victoria in place. A pewter charger with loose lavender, left, is our version of a room freshener, like the soup bowl with clove-pricked pomander balls, opposite. The collection of small burgundy cylindrical boxes, in the background, was designed for spices and fits in the larger box below.*

*A synthetic substance that can be cut to fit the bottoms of various-size flowerpots and other containers. When it's wet it's malleable, so that the stems of flowers can be pushed into it, but it's stiff enough to give young shoots and stems something to lean on. It's available at most gardening and flower stores. We usually keep it in the bottom of crocks used over and over again for arrangements.

199

In the kitchen at Muskettoe Pointe, crocks of herbs line a counterfeit counter faked with cutting boards (see Tools, page 75). A stainless-steel sink lies under the center board. The faucet is hidden by wooden trim and a diversionary hedgerow of thyme, savory, and lavender. The wooden shelves, above, are converted toolboxes. The family-size grater, to the left of them, hides an electrical outlet, as does the Victorian gentleman propped under the right-hand window. A tin herald of spring in the other window, left, showed up last Christmas, an un-claimed gift. Under her are a spongeware crock of sage and a plain one of santolina. (Both are reproductions, as are all these crocks, from a nearby pottery.) A stack of ironstone plates is the first sign of supper. The peppers don't count; they're pure decoration.

EASTER

Right: *The Easter Bunny cuddles three-week-old Cary Hunter, whose first Easter basket rests on the bench next to them. His glasses (a lot like Uncle Jimmie's!) give him a professorial look.*

Early on Easter morning, a strange repeating rhythm can be heard echoing from the direction of the entrance lane to Muskettoe Pointe Farm. "Da-Da-Da-Da-Da, Da-DaDa, Da-Da-Da-Da-Da, DADADA . . ." over and over again. Even the whippoorwills cease their constant cries to listen as the sing-song repetitions grow more confident, and as laughter mixes with a grown-up's directions—"Stay in line! . . . Look for paw prints! . . . Keep on hopping!" Then, the source of this early-morning ruckus appears—a colorful train of children hopping frantically from one foot to the other, totally out of step and tune, attempting to keep up with their tireless leader, Aunt Cary, who bunny-hops them annually down this springtime trail to look for signs of the Easter Bunny. As it nears its destination, the line disintegrates, scattering children to all parts of the riverside gardens bursting with tulips, daffodils, periwinkle, forsythia, and hidden Easter baskets. The older children, experienced hunters, help novices discover their baskets and comfort them when they spot a huge pair of white fuzzy ears and matching cotton tail—"the Easter Bunny!" In previous years he's sent his cousins—the Easter Chicken, above left, the Easter Frog, above right, and, once, an Easter Pig. This year he's come himself, wearing new glasses—an older, but wiser, Easter Bunny, left. He doesn't speak, just nods, shakes hands, and hugs; then he passes out our sweetest Easter tradition—chocolate-covered buttercream eggs made and personally monogrammed in icing by Liza (seen on previous page; recipe on page 214). Easter lunch will be served shortly in the herb garden, but until then it's hard to resist an hors d'oeuvre or two—those little yellow marshmallow chickens, chocolate bunnies, malted eggs, and jelly beans overflowing from the children's overstuffed baskets.

Left: *A view of Easter luncheon, starting with dessert—a big bowl of fresh strawberries, cream, and homemade shortcake. The normal procession would start at the other end, with a plate, silverware, and a festive pink napkin. (Dare we reveal the napkin's true identity? They're Grease Getters, cotton utility towels meant to cut it in the garage, not at the table.*) Help yourself to a slice of ham on a roll with herb butter, but pass on the eggs—they're wooden decorations. Pile on the cool, crispy marinated vegetables—zucchini, turnips, carrots, and asparagus. If you're quick, you won't miss the tomato aspic, but the way the temperature's rising it will soon be gazpacho. Last, but not least, try two kinds of salad—crab, on the left, and French red potato, on the right. The triple-trestled table was designed by Father after Mom's favorite—a noble seventeenth-century version exhibited in the American Wing at the Metropolitan Museum of Art in New York City. The pine-plank top rests on a pull-apart pegged frame that can be disassembled and stored when not in use.*

*Look for them in the car-maintenance departments of large discount stores. If you go for the dyed variety, wash separately—they run!

SHORTCUT SHORTCAKE

Buy a box of piecrust mix and follow directions on box. Roll out piecrust to ¼-inch thickness. Cut in squares and bake according to directions. Top with sweetened strawberries and whipped cream.

Opposite left: *A trio of salads—red potato, tomato aspic, and crab. Opposite right: Vegetables vinaigrette, served on a Mason's ironstone platter.*

Preceding illustration: *An Easter luncheon set up in the herb garden on a handmade trestle table, presided over by a large wooden rabbit, Elsie Dinsmore, and bordered by daisies in front and back, chive blooms on the right, and sage in the back.*

RED POTATO SALAD

You leave the skins on for flavor, for color, and because, of course, it's easier. Some like it warm—we like it cold.

5 pounds red potatoes
1 cup olive oil
⅓ cup wine vinegar
1 large garlic clove, finely chopped
1 teaspoon paprika
Lots of salt and red pepper to taste
2 tablespoons lemon juice

Scrub potatoes and place in salted boiling water. Cook about 25 minutes. Don't peel. Cool and slice. Combine remaining ingredients and toss with potatoes. Let stand 1 hour or more in the refrigerator if you're serving it cold.

Serves twenty.

CRABMEAT SALAD

1 cup mayonnaise*
1 cup sour cream
1 tablespoon grated onion
1 tablespoon lemon juice
¼ teaspoon red pepper
Dash of Tabasco sauce
1 tablespoon capers
Salt to taste
1 pound lump crabmeat

Mix first eight ingredients, then add gently to crabmeat. Serve with lettuce and tomatoes or avocados.

Serves four.

*We prefer Duke's, a Virginia grocery-store favorite less sweet than most.

VEGETABLES VINAIGRETTE

At this time of the year in Virginia, the only thing you could possibly pick fresh from the garden would be peas and spinach. So we picked out carrots, turnips, zucchini, and asparagus fresh from the grocery store's garden section. Pick your own, then peel, cut, blanch, and marinate in a simple vinaigrette sauce in the refrigerator overnight. For more color, add red and yellow squiggles of radish skin and lemon peel.

TOMATO ASPIC

There are many things to recommend tomato aspic besides its rich southern heritage. 1. It's seasonless—you'll find it on tables from Easter to Christmas. 2. It's a great stand-in when the real things aren't available. 3. Decorated with chives or a pretty lettuce border, it gives the table a great jolt of color. 4. It's low-calorie.

3¾ cups V-8 juice
1 cup celery chunks
1 medium onion, sliced
1 bay leaf
1 teaspoon whole cloves
1 teaspoon salt
1 or 2 lemons, sliced thin
¼ teaspoon white pepper
2 envelopes unflavored gelatin
¼ cup vinegar

Combine 3 cups of V-8 juice with following seven ingredients and bring to a boil. Lower heat and simmer 15 minutes. Soften gelatin in ¾ cup V-8 juice and vinegar. Strain hot mixture well, then pour over cold gelatin mixture. Stir until dissolved. Pour into a mold and chill until firm.

Serves eight.

Above: *Liza's cakes, fresh from the oven, before the extras—icing, glazes, fillings, fruits, and nuts—are added, cooling in assorted old and new cake molds and pans.*

Left: *A cake retrospective of Carter family favorites whipped up by wonder baker Liza (for the bride who baked fourteen cakes for her own wedding—not including the four-tiered wedding cake—this was nothing!) and presented as an extra added attraction to Easter luncheon. The earliest favorite, the gingerbread square served with lemon sauce, front row, center, dates back to childhood in the fifties (for some of us). But each of the six, served up on handcrafted grocery-store-bag doilies—the orange-lemon cake, back row, left; the chocolate pound cake, center; the caramel cake, right; the jam cake, front row, left; and the peach upside-down cake, right—has a special place in the memories and palates of all of us.*

CHOCOLATE POUND CAKE

1/2 cup vegetable oil
1 stick butter, softened
2 cups sugar
3 eggs
1/2 cup boiling water
2/3 cup unsweetened cocoa
2 cups flour
1 1/2 teaspoons baking soda
1 cup milk or buttermilk
1 teaspoon vanilla extract

Cream together oil, butter, and sugar. Beat until light and fluffy. Beat in eggs one at a time. Pour boiling water over cocoa and mix thoroughly. Sift together flour and baking soda and add alternately with cocoa and milk to butter/egg mixture. Add vanilla extract. Pour into a greased and floured Bundt pan. Bake in a preheated 350-degree oven 1 hour. Glaze with Chocolate Glaze.

Serves ten to fifteen.

CHOCOLATE GLAZE

4 ounces semisweet baking chocolate
2 ounces unsweetened baking chocolate
1/3 cup superfine sugar
2 teaspoons instant coffee dissolved in 1/2 cup boiling water
2 tablespoons butter

Melt chocolates in a double boiler over hot but not boiling water. Meanwhile, dissolve sugar in hot coffee. Add to melted chocolate and cook over medium heat until it reaches a boil. Stir until slightly thickened, about 5–7 minutes. Remove from heat, then add butter. Stir until blended.

SPICY APPLESAUCE CAKE

3 cups all-purpose flour, sifted
1 cup raisins
1 cup walnuts, coarsely chopped
2 teaspoons baking powder
1/2 teaspoon salt
2 teaspoons cinnamon
1/2 teaspoon ground cloves
1/2 teaspoon nutmeg
1 cup butter, softened
2 cups sugar
2 eggs
2 cups applesauce

Sprinkle 1/4 cup flour over raisins and walnuts; toss. Sift together remaining flour, baking powder, salt, cinnamon, and cloves. Cream butter; gradually add sugar. Beat in eggs one at a time. Add dry ingredients alternately with applesauce, ending with flour. Fold in raisins and nuts. Pour into 2 buttered and floured 8-inch or 9-inch pans. Bake in a preheated 350-degree oven 35–40 minutes. Cool in pan. Frost with Caramel Frosting.

Serves ten to fifteen.

CARAMEL FROSTING

1/2 cup butter
1 cup light brown sugar
1/4 cup evaporated milk
1 3/4 cups confectioner's sugar, sifted

Melt butter over medium-low heat. Blend in brown sugar and bring to a boil. Stir constantly 2 minutes. Add milk and stir until mixture comes to a boil; cook 1 minute. Remove from heat; cool. Slowly add confectioner's sugar, beating well.

PEACH UPSIDE-DOWN CAKE

8 tablespoons butter
1/2 cup light brown sugar
1/4 teaspoon nutmeg
3–4 peaches, peeled and sliced
1 1/3 cups flour
3/4 cup sugar
2 teaspoons baking soda
1/4 teaspoon salt
1/2 cup milk
1 teaspoon vanilla extract
2 eggs

Melt 4 tablespoons butter in a saucepan. Add brown sugar and nutmeg and blend well. Pour into the bottom of a buttered 8-inch springform pan. Arrange peach slices, slightly overlapping, on brown-sugar mixture. Sift together flour, sugar, baking soda, and salt. Cream remaining 4 tablespoons butter to soften, then add flour mixture, milk, and vanilla extract. Beat 2 minutes with an electric mixer at medium speed, then add eggs and beat well. Pour batter over peaches. Bake in a preheated 375-degree oven 35 minutes. Cool cake 10 minutes, then invert onto a serving platter. Let stand 2 minutes before removing the pan. Serve warm.

Serves ten.

GINGERBREAD

1 cup butter, softened
1¹/₂ cups light brown sugar
2 eggs, well beaten
³/₄ cup molasses
1¹/₂ teaspoons ground ginger
1¹/₂ teaspoons cinnamon
1 teaspoon nutmeg
1 teaspoon ground cloves
2³/₄ cups flour
1¹/₂ teaspoons baking powder
¹/₂ teaspoon salt
1 cup milk
¹/₄ cup hot water

Cream butter, sugar, and eggs. Stir in molasses and spices. Sift together flour, baking powder, and salt. Add flour mixture and milk alternately to butter mixture, beating well after each addition. Add hot water and mix well. Pour into a greased 13 × 9 × 2-inch baking pan. Bake in a preheated 350-degree oven 40–50 minutes.

Yields 36–40 squares.

LEMON SAUCE FOR GINGERBREAD

¹/₂ cup sugar
4 teaspoons cornstarch
¹/₄ teaspoon salt
1 cup water
2 tablespoons butter
1¹/₂ tablespoons lemon juice
1 teaspoon grated lemon rind

Combine sugar, cornstarch, and salt in a saucepan. Mix well. Add water and cook over low heat 5 minutes, until clear and thickened. Remove from heat and stir in butter, lemon juice, and lemon rind.

ORANGE-LEMON LAYER CAKE

2 cups sugar
1¹/₂ sticks butter, softened
4 ounces cream cheese
4 eggs, separated
2¹/₂ cups all-purpose flour
1 teaspoon baking powder
1 teaspoon baking soda
1 cup sour cream
¹/₂ cup orange juice
1 cup walnuts, ground
Zest of 2 oranges
Zest of 1 lemon

Cream together sugar, butter, and cream cheese. Add egg yolks one at a time, beating well after each addition. Sift together flour, baking powder, and baking soda. Add alternately with sour cream and orange juice to creamed mixture. Fold in walnuts and fruit zest. Beat egg whites until stiff. Fold into cake batter. Pour into 3 buttered and floured 8-inch or 9-inch pans. Bake in a preheated 350-degree oven 25–30 minutes. Cool on wire racks. Spread Lemon Buttercream between layers.

Serves ten to fifteen.

LEMON BUTTERCREAM

3 egg yolks
¹/₂ stick unsalted butter
4 teaspoons cornstarch
³/₄ cup sugar
2 teaspoons grated lemon rind
¹/₂ cup lemon juice
1¹/₂ cups heavy cream
¹/₄ cup confectioner's sugar

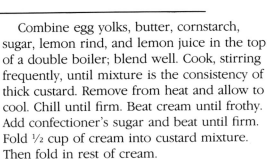

JAM CAKE

1 cup butter, softened
1 cup sugar
5 eggs
3 cups all-purpose flour
1 tablespoon cinnamon
¹/₂ teaspoon ground cloves
1 teaspoon allspice
1 teaspoon baking powder
1 teaspoon baking soda
1 cup buttermilk
³/₄ cup raspberry jam
³/₄ cup strawberry jam
³/₄ cup apricot jam
1 cup pecans, chopped

Cream together butter and sugar. Add eggs one at a time, beating well after each addition. Sift together flour, cinnamon, cloves, allspice, baking powder, and baking soda. Add alternately to batter with buttermilk and jams. Fold in pecans. Pour into a greased and floured Bundt pan. Bake in a preheated 350-degree oven 1 hour.

Serves ten to fifteen.

Combine egg yolks, butter, cornstarch, sugar, lemon rind, and lemon juice in the top of a double boiler; blend well. Cook, stirring frequently, until mixture is the consistency of thick custard. Remove from heat and allow to cool. Chill until firm. Beat cream until frothy. Add confectioner's sugar and beat until firm. Fold ¹/₂ cup of cream into custard mixture. Then fold in rest of cream.

Besides the bunny hop, the baskets, and the front-lawn egg toss, there is one more (mouth-watering) Easter tradition, started by Ga-Ga (and almost lost)—her annual presentation of chocolate-covered buttercream eggs, each with our name in icing on top, made by a wonderful Richmond confectioner. One Easter a glum Ga-Ga reported her Easter-egg source had closed shop. That was the year she passed the chocolate torch to Liza. Next Easter, the eggs were back (above, and page 202-3), one for each of us. Since then, eighteen years ago, the task has grown from nine eggs to forty!

EASTER EGGS

3 1-pound boxes confectioner's sugar
2 8-ounce packages cream cheese
¹/₂ pound butter, softened
1 teaspoon vanilla extract
12 ounces semisweet chocolate chips
3 ounces unsweetened chocolate

Cream together butter and cream cheese. Add sifted sugar 1 cup at a time. Add vanilla extract and mix well. Chill for several hours, until firm enough to form into eggs. (You may need to refrigerate again before coating with chocolate.) Melt chocolate in the top of a double boiler. Dip eggs one at a time in chocolate. (Liza usually uses a wooden spoon and a fork.) After dipping, place eggs on cookie sheet until chocolate hardens. These can be made a few days before Easter—just be sure to refrigerate until a couple of hours before you're ready to serve!

Yields 12 large eggs or 24 small ones.

A family-style Easter basket (not an annual event)—a laundry basket made into a carry-along bed for a very special Easter treat—a newborn grandchild.

Left: *Guest of honor at an Easter-egg hunt overlooking the Hudson, a dapperly clad, freckle-faced chocolate Easter bunny is doomed for dessert.*

Above: *Bunny hieroglyphics inscribed in the sand of Muskettoe Pointe's bunny trail by a nimble-fingered young artist, just out of sight, right.*

Preceding illustration: *Far from the warren (if there is such a thing for chocolate bunnies), Flopsy and Peter happily nestle into a Muskettoe Pointe substitute—a wooden dough tray cozied with dried grass and buttercups.*

Above: *A Muskettoe Pointe wreath of golden yarrow, pink globe amaranth, yellow and white statice, silvery sage leaves, lavender, and purple oregano grabbed off the wall at the last minute fits right over the crown of a beaten-up cowboy hat that won first prize at an Easter bonnet contest.*

Right: *Inverted, this deep straw hat could nest several swallow families. Right side up, it nests one shy little girl—Mary Randolph—who's considering it her Easter bonnet.*

In spring, as grass grows higher and the fields are cut, the children begin to listen for the clippety-clop of the team of miniature ponies that pulls Mr. Howard Atkins's pony cart. He stays only as long as it takes to fill it up with grass that will help feed the ponies during the winter. And then, to give the expectant children the treat they've been waiting for, he takes them for a ride around the farm in their own movable (sort of) Easter basket.

Above: *At the picket fence separating his ponies from tasty irises and English boxwood, Mr. Atkins steadies his ponies as passengers Emily and her brother John Christian hold on to their hats for the takeoff.*

Left: *"I can't believe it's over" could be the thought of a disconsolate John Christian, right, as he and Emily, left, stay put until they're told it really is time to get down. The pony-cart decoration, far right, is a child's plastic toy stuck there like a fancy coach lantern. There's a Santa in a sleigh right below it.*

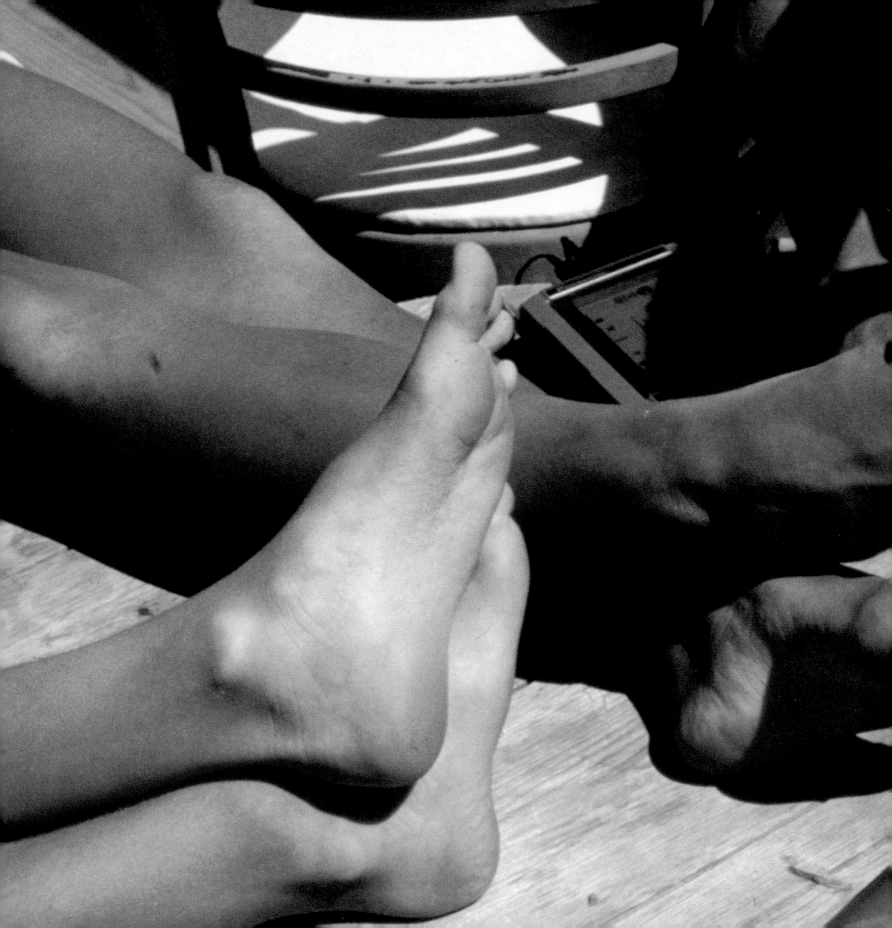

SUMMER

SUMMER

Through low-hanging branches, a glimpse of red, white, and blue greets guests to the Fourth of July at Muskettoe Pointe.

The parade from the house to the log cabin, led by a color guard of one, Emily, age two. She'll soon be followed by a crowd.

Time out to reread the words that proclaimed us free to enjoy "life, liberty, and the pursuit of happiness."

INDEPENDENTS

We enter summer celebrating independence—our nation's, our family's, and the special kind this season gives us. We light fireworks; revel in red, white, and blue; and display our modern-day patriotism with old-fashioned zeal. At Muskettoe Pointe Farm it's the same. A riverside picnic kicks off the day with flags flying everywhere. A miniature color guard of grandchildren parades picnickers to the log-cabin site. Others follow, dragging tables, chairs, benches, platters of food, baskets of bread, cookies, pewter plates, mugs, pitchers of lemonade,

and lots of ice. There are vegetables and herbs fresh-picked from the garden, crabs netted from the river, and frozen custard churned by hand. In the spirit of the day, we join in patriotic song, listen to a reading of the Declaration of Independence, and, after sunset, watch America's birthday candles light up the sky. Later, there'll be a marshmallow roast and hunts for lightning bugs, snipes, and missing shoes. Later still, there'll be journeys back and forth to the house, arms laden with picnic leftovers and sleeping children.

Left: *Who needs a flagpole? We fly our flag from the log-cabin door—a Stars and Stripes entrance to an American summer.*

A homespun picnic on a sturdy pine table in front of the log cabin. Left to right: fried chicken, tomatoes and broccoli, a crock of lemonade, steamed crabs, a basket of bread, and cold pasta salad. In keeping with our celebration, we fly the British Union Jack, America's Stars and Stripes, and a Virginia State flag.

FRIED CHICKEN

With so much good fast-food chicken around, sometimes you just don't want to bother. When you do . . .

6 pieces chicken (you choose)
1 cup all-purpose flour
½ teaspoon salt
½ teaspoon black pepper
1 teaspoon baking powder
Vegetable oil

Shake the chicken in a big paper bag with the flour, salt, pepper, and baking powder. Heat 1 inch of oil in a large frying pan and fry chicken 10 minutes on each side or until well browned.

Serves four, depending on appetites.

STEAMED CRABS

No plates, just newspaper on the table and lots of hot butter and Horseradish Sauce; recipe given below. Pick and dip.

2 cans beer
3 cups white vinegar
2 dozen crabs
Old Bay seafood seasoning*

To prepare the crabs, you'll need a 16-quart steamer or to do as we do—push chicken wire in the bottom of a big enamel pot to keep the crabs off the bottom. Bring beer and vinegar to a boil, then reduce the heat and add crabs. Sprinkle with seasoning and steam about 15 minutes.

Serves eight.

*Available at some grocery stores and fish markets, or substitute Lawry's Seasoned Salt.

HORSERADISH SAUCE

1 cup catsup
½ cup horseradish
1 tablespoon lemon juice
Salt to taste

Combine all ingredients. Sometimes it's best to leave the proportions to individual taste.

Left: *An old wooden dough tray lined with a giant plastic garbage bag and ice serves up frosty cans of beer and soda. A barelegged child plays tag in the background.*

Bottom: *For a help-yourself meal (left to right): the dough tray of drinks, red-and-white checked napkins cut from the same fabric that covers the chair seats, two pileups of ironstone plates (Mom insists, no matter how informal the meal, that food looks and tastes better on real plates), open liters of wine, pewter chalices, and mugs of silverware.*

COLD PASTA SALAD

Perfect for our Fourth of July crowd or any big gathering. Easy to do in large quantities, and easy to improvise.

1 pound cappellini (very thin spaghetti), cooked al dente and drained
1 cup each broccoli florets and whole snow peas, cooked but crisp
1/2 cup sliced almonds, sautéed until golden
1 cup ripe olives, sliced
1/2 cup green onion, chopped
2 4-ounce jars pimiento, chopped
Vegetable oil

Cool spaghetti and toss with a small amount of oil. Add remaining ingredients, then toss with the dressing, given below. Place in a tightly sealed container and chill in the refrigerator overnight.

Serves ten.

COLD PASTA DRESSING

1/2 cup white vinegar
1 cup olive oil
4 cloves garlic, finely minced
Salt and pepper to taste

Combine all ingredients. Shake well and pour over pasta.

ALMOST-HOMEMADE MAYONNAISE

A tasty topping for pasta or any salad.

2 cups Duke's mayonnaise*
1 cup sour cream
1 tablespoon lemon juice
Salt
Red pepper
Paprika

Mix mayonnaise and sour cream. Season with lemon juice, salt, and red pepper. Add paprika for color.

*See page 209.

FROZEN CUSTARD

Recipe #1, when you want a lot of it—outdoors and old-fashioned. Recipe #2, when you want a little—indoors and easy. (Both recipes produce hard custard, the consistency of regular ice cream.)

Recipe #1
2 quarts milk
6 eggs
2 cups sugar
2 tablespoons all-purpose flour
Pinch of salt
1 cup heavy cream
1 teaspoon vanilla extract

Scald milk in a saucepan. Beat eggs well; then add sugar, flour, and salt. When milk coats the back of a spoon, add egg mixture; turn off heat and stir until well mixed. Cool thoroughly. Add cream and vanilla extract. Pour mixture into the can of a 1-gallon ice-cream freezer; freeze according to directions.

Serves twelve.

Recipe #2
2 cups milk
3 eggs
1/3 cup sugar
2 teaspoons vanilla extract
Pinch of salt

Heat milk in a bowl in a microwave oven 4 minutes, or until scalded. Beat eggs well, then add sugar and mix. Pour milk into the egg-and-sugar mixture. Heat on high, uncovered, 8–10 minutes, stirring after 5 minutes. When mixture coats the back of a spoon, remove from oven. Add vanilla extract and salt. Freeze, stirring occasionally, about 4 hours.

Note: This recipe was written for a 500-watt microwave oven. Adjust cooking time up or down, depending on your oven wattage.

Serves three.

Above: *Serve-yourself salad: tomatoes and broccoli topped with "Antarctica."*

Herbs aren't the only things grown at Muskettoe Pointe Farm. By the Fourth of July, the garden at left is providing tomatoes like those seen above. Benie Robins, the creator of the scarecrow and the "scarecans" tied around the fence perimeter, puts in plants and seeds starting in April. "We grow only big things," Mom says. "That way you can go out and pick a whole meal very quickly. Little things like butter beans and snaps take too long to pick." One exception—the peas, far left: "They died a natural death"; followed by prosperous rows of lettuce, squash, cabbage, beets, eggplants, and tomatoes.

ANTARCTICA

Because it sort of looks like that and tastes great served icy cold over any fresh summer vegetable.

2 cups cottage cheese
2 tablespoons sour cream
2 tomatoes, peeled and chopped
¹/₂ cup chopped green pepper
1 medium onion, grated
Seasoned salt to taste
Tabasco sauce to taste

Combine all ingredients. Or, instead of peeling and chopping tomatoes, scoop out their insides, add pulp to other ingredients, refill tomato shells, and serve.

Getaways

There are two kinds of getaways—the places you go for change and the changes you make without going. If you don't have the first, you can invent it with the second—cook outside instead of in, dress up your bed in driftwood and lace, cluster delicate seashells in tiny bowls.

Muskettoe Pointe was always the summer getaway for those of us who'd left it behind. But not for my parents, who found theirs on the Outer Banks of North Carolina. We stay with them or near them in rented getaways of our own. We share cottages and cooking, hammocks and makeshift beds. We call our clotheslines closets, and collect a new breed of household pet and the finest paper-plate art. We celebrate birthdays, borrow each other's books, and lose our shoes. On the last day we pack up our summer totems—shells, driftwood, weathered chairs, pets, bottlecaps, art, and kids—and hope they'll make the magic last until next year.

Top: *Royal example of summer's finest beach architecture—a sand castle flying a banner of sea grass and reeds.* Middle: *A favorite summer getaway silhouetted by a young artist.* Left: *Drift Wood Cottage, one of the more colorful landmarks along the Outer Banks.*

Above: *Summer after summer this old oceanfront inn welcomes back the families (ours among them) and the other guests who appreciate its simple luxuries: a sandy beach, help-yourself beach umbrellas, wrap-* *around porches, grandstand views, rocking chairs galore, a cranky old ice machine, one pay phone, a cast-iron skillet on every stove, and lots of free postcards to color in on a rainy day.*

Right: *Quick getaway to easy summer living and dining—a long, slinky porch. A large picnic table and lots of chairs give bare-foot cousins front-row seats on summer.*

Left: *At Bodie Island since 1872—one of the four light-houses of the Outer Banks, hori-zontally striped in black and white. A security light that shines all night!*

233

WEATHERS

Sunburnt cottages, docks, and doorways; battalions of driftwood, shells, beach grasses, and bottles lost and found along America's shoreline—they're summer's flotsam and jetsam—bleached, buffeted, polished, and smoothed by wind, sun, salt water, and spray, worn down by miles at sea—we swipe them up like bargains in a basement; beach booty, our free souvenirs to save and give our summer homes a simple kind of majesty.

Left: *Almost adrift, Drift Wood Cottage has earned its name. It was a getaway for the same family for years and years, and we were all jealous until they decided to rent it to families like us—for two summers running. The best fishing, crabbing, swimming, and sunsets lay right out the back door. So did romance—Christian and Chris announced their engagement out there! It was our candy-colored, floating fantasy island until a storm last summer took it away.* Above: *Stuck for a vase? Walk down the beach and find a stoic beauty like this rusting paint can. Check for tears and holes, abrade with rough cloth, rinse, and let dry. For outdoor exhibition only.*

Weathery walls and open-air shelves, salvaged from an old hotel, build character into this beach-cottage kitchen.

Sun-ripened wood, shells, and peaches bide their time outside a cottage door.

A sideboard constructed from a boat-hatch cover and supported by two lobster traps.

Summer portables—music, meals, and all-weather furniture.

The no-paint patina of this vintage cottage comes from quality outdoor aging.

A shingled facade studded with seafaring names and shipwreck memorabilia.

Outdoor eating and/or seating provided by a faded pair of summer settle tables.

Summer throwaways—two washed-up crates stacked into an instant end table and lit by a lamp with a driftwood base.

Collected on a bedroom dresser, silhouetted against a bamboo shade (left to right), a beach bottle with drift-wood twigs, a striped summer purse, a tin box—a safeguard for fragile summer finds—a radio on top of a summer read, bayberry branches in a coffee-can vase, a pastel-tinted postcard, a roll of kite string, a tube of lip balm, and favorite summer jewelry in a paisley case on top of a paper-plate party invitation.

On summer beaches, with little else to pick, we gather shells—buckets of them, T-shirts full. They fall from tiny pockets at night, leave sandy trails along window-sills and shelves, prop up books, line our stairs, collect in a million broken heaps outside cottage doors. Though they are the abandoned homes of sea snails, we rarely think of them as that. Instead, they're summer marbles, tiny baubles, gems washed up from some seaweed-covered treasure chest many fathoms deep.

Top: *Heaped like fruit in a wooden bowl—pinecones and whelks.*

Middle: *A summer showcase of all kinds of shells, wrapped around original artworks, and an incongruous collection of family finds.*

Bottom: *A mosaic of shell fragments embedded in three cement steps to the shore.*

*Tiny shells, like buds, no larger
than a child's thumbnail, nest in an
ironstone dish watched over by a wood-
en sheep—astray from a miniature flock.*

Top: *Whelks climb a cottage staircase.*

Middle: *A fishy watercolor swims
inside a natural habitat of sand
and shells. To make, cut out
four pieces of cardboard in
swirly shapes, glue at corners,
and brush perimeter with
gesso primer. Position shells
and sprinkle with fine sand.
Picture is attached with mask-
ing tape on the back.*

Bottom: *Ring around the rosemary (left)
and santolina (right).*

SUMMER

BEDS

I n summer we want beds stripped down to good views and breezes, white cotton sheets, spareness, bareness. We want the feeling of sleeping outside when we're sleeping in, so we shove our beds next to windows, drape them in driftwood and linen, spread them with pale, faded colors, pile up pillows for headboards—good books, good nights.

Left: *Bed with a view—ocean by day, stars by night—built on a deck in a day (no springs!) and surrounded by (left to right): child's watercolor on bedside crate, fishnet flounce, airplane whirligig, decoy, Indian print pillows and spread, shell bookmark, sea sculpture, child's twig rocker, and army blanket for cool nights. It's strong enough to support all kinds of frolicking twosomes—pint-sized (Sam and Christian, bottom) and romanticized (John and Liza, top). Another summer sleeper: a hammock swinging from a cottage porch (second from top), cradling a tiny rocker (third from top).*

Preceding illustrations: *In summer, there's no such thing as an empty hammock. It's a snoozer, library, playground, bedroom for a last-minute guest. Just roll it out, hook it up, and jump in fast! Top inset: Bedroom extender for kids or a full house—two tents pitched right outside the cottage door. Bottom inset: Sweet dreams are made of this—lots of good pillows.*

Above: *Driftwood pilings from a dilapidated fence were tugged from a tangle of bay-side vines to transform Mom and Dad's once ordinary brass bed in North Carolina into this bower of sensuous delights. A faux-batik bed sheet was sacrificed to drape the back rail. The water lilies floating silently above, found for $5, reflect the mauvey roses of the pillowcases below. A nightstand, left, holds a bamboo shelf tucked with dried roses and cinnamon sticks, a doll named Irma (a daughter's gift), a sewing basket, and a well-worn red hat.*

Top left: *Head-to-toe windows are the only luxury of Cary's spartan summer bedroom.*

Bottom left: *Behind a plaid curtain at Drift Wood lurks a hideaway bed Jane Eyre would have loved—solitary, sunlit, with water views all around.*

Top right: *Curled up for warmth, two brothers sleep under favorite babyhood blankets.*

Bottom right: *Howard and book on a bed of calico vines.*

Above: *Dressed up for summer in white cotton eyelet, our bed in the city, a cousin of the one at left, was built by Dad and me from one wide pine plank fitted between two driftwood trapstakes. The frame's the standard metal kind on wheels that's rolled away for an occasional underbed clear-out. (See unmade version at right for a better look.) The oversize French-cut pillows (put away at night) convert "cozy" to "cool" during warm months.*

Top right: *As in an Andrew Wyeth painting, a lace curtain lifts lightly over a pastel-colored bed in our upstate New York retreat. The pink-and-white candy-cane striped seersucker spread was bought second-hand; the polished-cotton pillow has been mellowed by the sun.*

Bottom left: *The iron bedstead is softened by a trio of eyelet doilies.*

Bottom right: *A wider view reveals the perfect summer sleeper.*

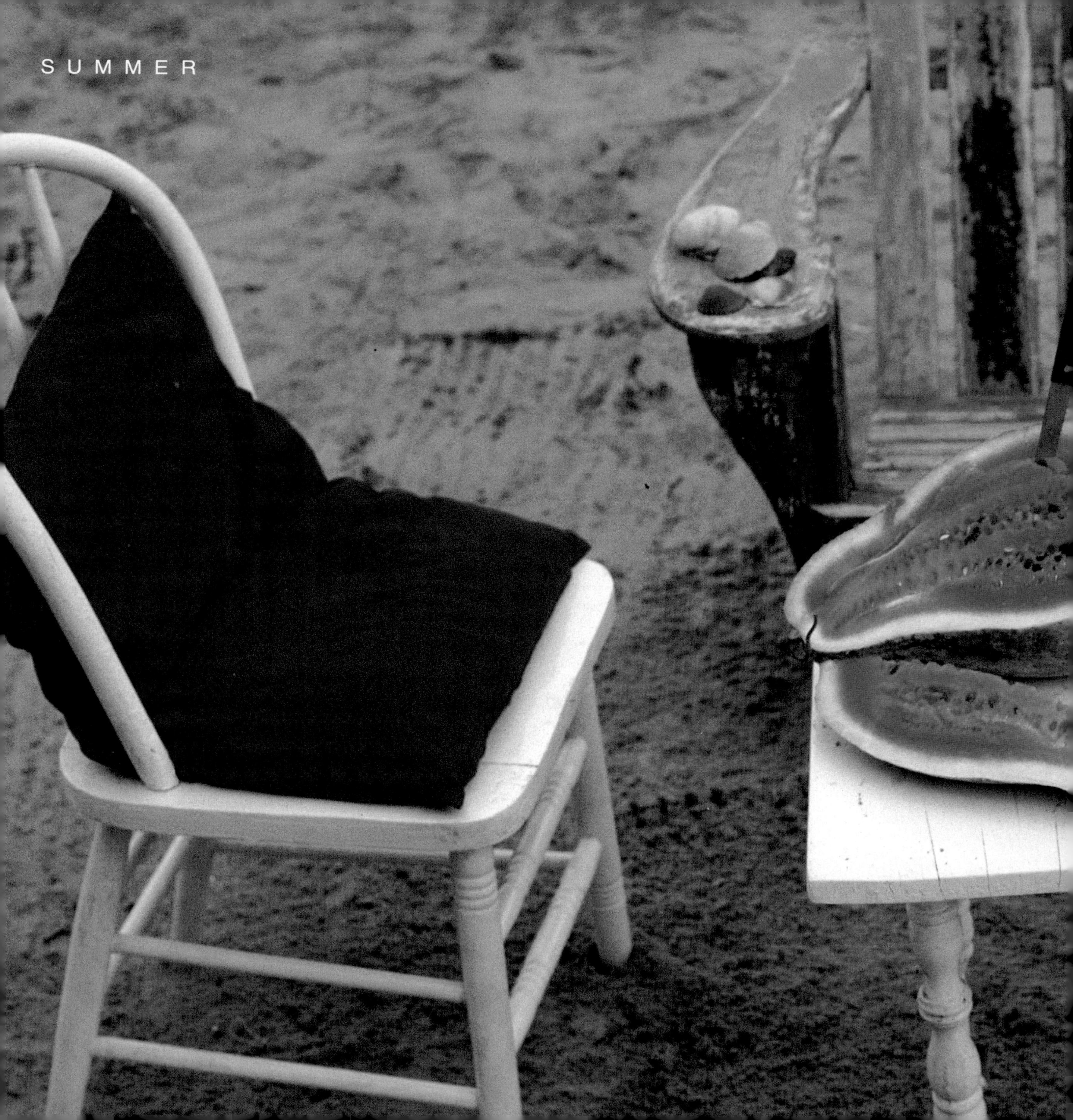

SEATING

Welcome beneath this roof of mine!
Welcome! this vacant chair is thine...

Henry Wadsworth Longfellow graciously welcomes the ghost of a departed poet with this greeting in his poem "Robert Burns." In summer, when chairs are at a premium, we improvise. We scavenge a madcap variety, paint, patch, cover, and cushion them, and hope when our ghosts or guests appear, they'll find one that suits them just right.

Preceding illustration: *A feast of watermelon and chairs—two punched up with glossy color, one peeled down to rainbow layers.*

Above: *Hot seat for a wet bottom—a good old rocker, ready for anything summer can dish out.*

Above: *An armless armchair, rehabilitated with a stretchy white knit.* Above right: *"Old chairs never die..." This one hangs out in Duck, North Carolina.* Right: *A congregation of porch sitters can find room on this old pew.*

Above left: *Backyard chair in a city home, nicknamed "Gumby."*

Above right: *An overexposed bowback gets a rag-rug seat.*

Left: *Many a high tide has beached this displaced park bench and cable table.*

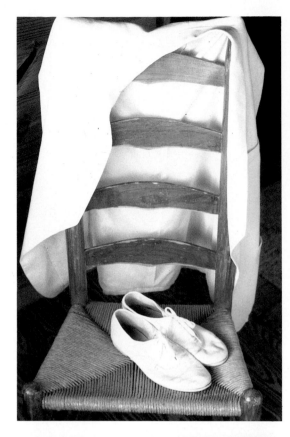

Top: *Never give up on rickety chairs. When straw seats give way, plug them up with planks cut to fit.*

Above: *There's always room for one more when the table's round and the seat's a bench. On the terrace at Muskettoe Pointe, a retopped butcher block, a one-planker, and single seating for two.*

Top: *In the mountains, we view our sunsets from a mountain classic like an Adirondack chair.*

Above: *At the beach, when the sun drops behind that line of blue, we reserve a rocker... sometimes two. Joined by a third, below, this family of rockers has a grandstand view.*

Top left: *Sophisticated rocker—a rush-bottomed ladderback in sport coat and jazzy shoes.*

Left: *Uncouth cousin to the chair above, a colorful survivor of life on the outside.*

Above: *Like summer tapestries, a khaki shirt and a kimono decorate a wooden wall at the hotel.*

Below: *From wall to bed rail, a flowery kimono adds romance, color, and a taste of Matisse to a summer atelier on the Outer Banks.*

Early Americans hung their clothes on pegs. In summer, we mimic them with clothespinned lines, hangers, and hooks. Our wardrobes are scant—T-shirts and shorts. We stack them up like pancakes on shelves shared with books.

Left: *Paperbacks make room for stacks of T-shirts, shorts, and summer spreads.*

Below: *A summer banner, brightly colored bathing trunks, welcomes guests to a party.*

Below: *Summer whites on a wall and a chair, illuminated by a slatted sunset.*

CLOSETS

SUMMER

Straw

W

When the wolf's at the door, you may reconsider (like the three little pigs) having a house of straw, but for hats and mats and a wide variety of summer constructions there's no sturdier stuff.

Clockwise from upper left: *We store our mallets, wickets, and balls in a basket so we can tote them easily from house to car to yard; a child's summer chest of drawers brimming with clothes and funny collections; four fans, strung together, shade a beach-house bulb; an Indian doll couple make a seat out of a hand-painted basket; bamboo shades cool down our sunny hotel loft for a quiet midday read; a light- weight suitcase with a removable tray dis- plays prized postcards and notepaper at home or away; we hit the beach with toys, tubes, towels, magazines, and cups—a basket at the end of the day helps scoop them up; at Muskettoe Pointe, fresh-picked squash is left out in baskets to be seen and enjoyed; a straw mat at Drift Wood's door spells out a welcome to a favorite spot; a coffee-can vase gets a straw overcoat on Mom and Dad's dining-room table.*

Left: *An off-duty brimmer decorates a straw-colored siding in the Outer Banks. Baskety catchall, below it, stems a tide of towels, linens, dribs and drabs. The chair seat is woven straw.*

Preceding illustration and center right: *Two Mad Hatters, Sam and Carter, take turns under a roomy Panama.*

SUMMER

Black-and-white pig meets crow on a red-and-white checkered tablecloth.

Plywood tribute to the infamous "nag" of Nags Head, North Carolina.

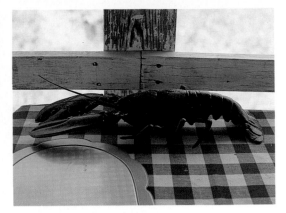

Escaped from a plate? No, just a plastic lobster centerpiece.

PETS

Not what you think—no dogs or cats or gerbils even—we had plenty of those real kinds of pets growing up (Saint Bernards, Siamese cats, a parakeet named Ernie, a rabbit named Flea, and the burro and horses already mentioned). Our summer menagerie is different—fantastic facsimiles to collect, to startle and surprise. The handiwork of weekend whittlers, artists of a different bent, displayed at roadside galleries and in jumbled junkyards through-

Birds of a feather: along a beach highway, above, a goose that gathers mail for the wood-carver Charles Reber and, left, a birthday "quacker" (made by Mom for an enthusiastic grandson) born in the U.S.A.

out the Outer Banks of North Carolina (our summer territory), they transform our station wagons into four-wheeled Noah's arks. (They're perfect companions for the places we rent that have ruled out the red-blooded kind.) We take them home and set them free to fly, perch, roam, and scatter to unexpected corners of our summer roosts. They are fine substitute companions until we return to the real things—yelping and chirping and licking their greetings.

From Drift Wood's entranceway swings a peach-colored parrot welcoming arriving guests (right). A spunky straw donkey (far right) carries a cargo of shells.

Left: *Swooping seagulls of painted plywood identify an Outer Banks beach house.*

Bottom left: *A surrealistic surprise at the top of the stairs—a shadowy crow perched on a make-believe fence of driftwood treasures. Above, a straw hat streams a stars-and-stripes trail.*

Below: *Pieces of driftwood can remind us, as can clouds, of more substantial things, like a goose's torso and a long, skinny neck. Charles Reber helped this piece along somewhat with a saw.*

Right: *The side of Charles Reber's weather-beaten cottage becomes a bulletin board for all manner of seagoing subjects (left to right): a swan behind a pecking crow, a flotilla of diving whales dodging floating oars, and a shipwrecked bedstead leaning against a bottle-crate "cupboard"; a white crab-pot float, like a seaside softball, dangles above.*

Top: *A steadfast turtle, carved out of a single hunk of wood, as delicately painted as the water-colored fig behind it.*

Above: *A portrait of the artist Bob Wallace and his "oinkers." The familiar shape of the smaller pig is a soda bottle metamorphosed with cement. The cement "mama" and her litter standing in a wooden trough probably weigh close to what a real pig family weighs.*

SUMMER

FOOD

The scene: The hot, frantic kitchen at Muskettoe Pointe. Company's coming—the line at the sink is ten deep. An impatient Aunt Nancy, with mushrooms to rinse, heads out the back door. Without hesitating, she plunks the mushrooms right down on the bricks (see preceding illustration), turns on the spigot, and douses the mushrooms with a stream from the garden hose. Mission accomplished, and precedent set for the lighthearted mood of the summer food that follows.

Above and right: *Lemony remains of a beach-side lunch—Icebox Shrimp (recipe below) and big yellow cups.*

Left: *The little drawing, artist unknown, depicts a great end-of-day catch from the waters of the Outer Banks. Brother-in-law Hunter has taught us all the patience required for ocean fishing, and shared with us the joys and rewards of his special seafood recipes. Catch one, below left.*

HUNTER'S BLUEFISH WITH HORSERADISH SAUCE

True to his name, Hunter is the great sportsman of the family. Every summer on the Outer Banks, he not only catches the fish but cooks them, too. His bluefish dinner has become a summer tradition.

1 cup sour cream
¹/₂ cup horseradish (less or more, to taste)
2 tablespoons lemon juice
1 teaspoon capers
1¹/₂ pounds bluefish, filleted
Salt and pepper
3 tablespoons butter
Lemon slices, parsley, and chives to taste

In a bowl, combine sour cream, horseradish, lemon juice, and capers. Sprinkle the fish with salt and pepper. Melt butter in a 13 × 9 × 2-inch baking dish. Remove from heat, then turn fish over in the butter, coating both sides. Pour sour cream mixture over fish and bake, uncovered, in a preheated 350-degree oven 25 minutes or until fish flakes. Garnish with parsley, chives, and lemon slices.

Serves four. (If you double the recipe, don't double the horseradish.)

ICEBOX SHRIMP

Mother would make a vat of this and keep it in the refrigerator. It had a pungent smell and a pungent taste—like summer itself. It was mainly served as an appetizer, but we'd always pile it on saltines and end up making a meal of it.

5 pounds shrimp, peeled and cooked
3 large onions, sliced into rings
2 lemons, sliced razor thin

Put shrimp, onion rings, and lemon slices in a flat pan and cover with marinade. Marinate in refrigerator at least 8 hours, stirring occasionally. Serve cold.

Serves twenty to twenty-five as an appetizer.

MARINADE

1¹/₂ cups oil
1 cup vinegar
1 tablespoon salt
1 dozen peppercorns
1 tablespoon celery seed
1 teaspoon sugar
6 bay leaves

Shake all ingredients well in a tightly covered 1-quart container. Pour over shrimp.

ICY SEAFOOD SERVING BOWL

Mom had read about this icy creation somewhere and, the night before a seafood party, decided to give it a try.

Take two plastic mixing bowls, one two sizes smaller than the other, and place the smaller one—filled with water—inside the larger one. Fill in the gap between the bowls—about an inch and a half—with seashells of all shapes and sizes, then fill with water. We placed four large oyster shells that extended beyond the rim of the bowl an equal distance apart for a more interesting design effect. Freeze overnight and unmold just before you plan to serve. Fill with fresh seafood or let it simply decorate your table. Ours, left, lasted for a couple of hours in bright sunlight, resting in a grapevine wreath stuck with bayberry twigs on a wooden block backed with driftwood.

CHILLED ZUCCHINI SOUP

A recipe from our cousin Trudi, who's usually supplying us with songs. Her tribute to an unsung vegetable.

2 13³/₄-ounce cans chicken broth
5 medium zucchini, sliced
4 medium onions, chopped
2 cloves garlic, sliced
¹/₂ teaspoon salt
1 cup Duke's mayonnaise*
2 teaspoons lemon juice
¹/₂ teaspoon ground nutmeg

Place 1 can of broth and the next four ingredients in a 3-quart saucepan. Bring to a boil over high heat, then reduce to a simmer. Cover and simmer 10 minutes or until vegetables are tender; cool. Place half the soup into a blender. Blend until smooth and pour into a bowl. Do the same with the other half, then combine them and stir in the second can of broth and the remaining ingredients. Cover and chill overnight.

Serves eight.

*See page 209.

267

PICASSOS

Right: *Dream house of acrylics on gesso-primed cardboard.**

Far right: *Annual summer art show exhibited on a kitchen bar. Prizes for the most talent, wackiness, imagination, realism, surrealism—everyone wins!*

Below: *The end of a birthday treasure hunt—a pirate's chest decorated with Magic Markers and stickers, and filled with candy and prizes.*

*Gesso: a thick white primer to smooth tough surfaces like the cardboard pictured here.

Left: *An original, signed and dated, by C.L.B.—of poster paint on paper plate, mounted on gesso-primed cardboard, and hung with kite string.*

Right: *Watercolor waves surrounded by a flowered robe, a paper-plate invitation, a Polaroid, a postcard, and a favorite wine label.*

Far right: *Teamwork— by at least a dozen hands—created this poster-paint masterpiece on reinforced cardboard.*

G

obs and globs and smears of unre-
strained, extravagant color! Summer gives
us that; so does a child's hand.

*For rainy days, parties, art shows with prizes—just provide space
(beaches are spill-proof—see previous page) and lots of tools: disposa-
ble brushes, jelly-glass dippers, stacks of paper and paper plates, any
kind of cardboard—from shirt backs to boxes—and a smorgasbord
of color—watercolors, poster paints, squishy tubes of acrylics, chalks,
crayons, colored pencils, Magic Markers. Add sand for texture, and
glue, tape, scissors, strips of old fabric, and string for finishing up.
Make room for masterpieces.*

A fringe of children in personalized T-shirts (nightgowns for some), done by hand with a permanent marking pen on extra-large Fruit-of-the-Looms.

LIST OF RECIPES

Special thanks to Liza, responsible for many of
the goodies below.